PRAISE FOR *LEADING THE FAMILY BUSINESS THROUGH SUCCESSION*

"Successful family enterprises that are able to thrive over generations don't 'just happen'; they are *led*. But what does leadership mean in the context of a family enterprise? How do leaders in both generations collaborate to transition the enterprise responsibly and in a way that sustains trust? This book provides useful answers to these fundamental questions and fills an important void in the family enterprise literature. Harry Korine and Michael Hilb understand that succession should always be viewed as an opportunity for strategic renewal that must balance continuity and change and that requires leadership from *both* generations. They provide informative cases and offer practical guidelines for leaders about how they can best play their roles and handle the tricky psychological, organizational and governance issues associated with succession. I recommend this book wholeheartedly."
Ivan Lansberg, Founding Partner, Lansberg, Gersick and Associates, USA.

"My company has been a key player in the automation sector since 1967. In the corporate landscape, personal destinies often intertwine with strategic decisions, sometimes leading to challenges in decision-making or interpreting complex situations. This book succeeds in restoring clarity where emotions might otherwise cloud judgment, thanks to the pragmatic approach and profound insight of its authors. With 25 years of experience in this field and a decade of managing the family business, I can attest to the value of the lessons shared in this book. My years of collaboration with my father have been a great gift, both personally and professionally, and the issues addressed by the authors are essential for understanding how these overlaps can be harnessed to maximize their value."
Raffaella Zavattaro, Chair, GEFIT SpA, Italy

"At a time when family businesses are grappling with the dual challenges of preserving their legacy and embracing change, *Leading the Family Business Through Succession* emerges as an important read. It succinctly captures the intricate dynamics of intergenerational leadership, providing essential guidance

for those navigating this complex terrain. The book offers a balanced approach to succession, emphasizing the valuable contributions that both generations bring, despite their differences. It is particularly relevant not only to Asian families like ours but also to family businesses globally."
Andy Lim, Chairman, Tembusu Partners, Singapore

"This is an insightful and valuable book for multiple generations. It's the perfect roadmap for families to sustain their business for the long term, providing best practice examples of how to structure governance to preserve the family while also creating value for all shareholders. It is very relevant for our third generation to embrace, learn from and implement."
Wissam Ariss, Vice Chairman, Unigaz Group, Lebanon, and Vice Chairman, Lumière Group, Lebanon

"In the family business, an effective succession process involves several generations working together, side by side. This indispensable book traces the route to follow and specifies the steps to be taken."
Pierre-Yves Gomez, Founder, French Corporate Governance Institute

"The big risk of family business remains succession. Harry Korine and Michael Hilb present succession not as a hierarchical issue, where at some point the current generation passes the lead to the next one, but as a collaborative one focused on both generations joining in value creation with their respective views and experiences, skills, and talents. This reframing not only fully fits our time but is a most welcome contribution as collaboration is a journey that must be initiated. This book provides practical tools and frameworks that will concretely help the family engage in this collaborative exercise. I highly recommend the book to any family that wants to be more collaborative, so as to be more sustainable and performing, as a family and as a business."
Ludo van der Heyden, Professor Emeritus, INSEAD

"Harry Korine and Michael Hilb offer a successful mix of approaches: practical examples, conceptual analyses, and thought-provoking exercises. This combination provides valuable guidance and support for family businesses navigating the challenges of generational transition."
Marie-Christine von Pezold, Independent Family Governance Adviser and Director, Family Business Network Switzerland

"This must-read book provides family officers and expert advisers with lessons they can apply to successful co-evolutions of generational succession in practice. Having led and advised family businesses in multiple geographic and cultural contexts for over three decades, I know this book will positively enrich your approaches to side by side cross-generational transitions."
Roderik J P Strobl, TEP, CEO, Leo Trust Switzerland

"Harry Korine and Michael Hilb provide invaluable insights, practical strategies and real-world examples that will be of interest to both the current and next generation of family business leaders. Whether you are preparing for a smooth transition or facing the challenges of succession, this book is a must-read as it provides the tools and knowledge you need to ensure the long-term success and legacy of your family business. Highly recommended for anyone who wants to preserve their family's entrepreneurial spirit"
Peter Vogel, Professor of Family Business and Entrepreneurship and Director of the Global Family Business Center, IMD

"As a co-owner of a Ukrainian second-generation family business, I found this book both exciting and highly educational. When my brother and I took over the business from our father after his sudden passing, we realized the importance of having a proper governance structure in place – something we lacked at that critical moment. This experience has driven me to ensure that the succession process for our next generation is smoother and well-prepared. The book's well-structured blend of family stories and practical advice makes it a valuable resource. Its practical guidelines and exercises are easy to apply, helping us build a strong governance structure while allowing Next Gens the freedom to pursue their own career aspirations. This perspective shift from succession to co-evolution has been truly eye-opening."
Olena Vovk, Co-owner, Enzym PJSC and Kormotech LLC, Ukraine

"This book is a gem in the vast literature on family business successions. I strongly support the view advocated by the authors that successions are not transactions but transitions, which require mutual role adjustment, collaboration, and open conversations between the generations. Combining conceptual models, short case studies, and drawing from real-life experiences the book is a highly enjoyable read. I strongly recommend it to you."
Thomas Zellweger, Chair of Family Business, University of St Gallen

Leading the Family Business Through Succession

How different generations create value together

Harry Korine and Michael Hilb

KoganPage

First published in Great Britain and the United States in 2025 by Kogan Page Limited

2nd Floor, 45 Gee Street
London
EC1V 3RS
United Kingdom

8 W 38th Street, Suite 902
New York, NY 10018
USA

www.koganpage.com

Kogan Page books are printed on paper from sustainable forests.

ISBNs

Hardback 978 1 3986 1712 4
Paperback 978 1 3986 1710 0
Ebook 978 1 3986 1711 7

British Library Cataloguing-in-Publication Data

A CIP record for this book is available from the British Library.

Library of Congress Cataloging-in-Publication Data
Names: Korine, Harry, 1962- author. | Hilb, Michael, author.
Title: Leading the family business through succession : how different generations create value together / Harry Korine and Michael Hilb.
Description: London, United Kingdom ; New York, NY, USA : Kogan Page, 2024. | Includes bibliographical references and index.
Identifiers: LCCN 2024031658 | ISBN 9781398617100 (paperback) | ISBN 9781398617124 (hardback) | ISBN 9781398617117 (ebook)
Subjects: LCSH: Family-owned business enterprises–Succession.
Classification: LCC HD62.25 .K67 2024
LC record available at https://lccn.loc.gov/2024031658

Typeset by Integra Software Services, Pondicherry
Print production managed by Jellyfish
Printed and bound by CPI Group (UK) Ltd, Croydon CR0 4YY

CONTENTS

LIST OF FIGURES

Introduction

Leading the family business through succession: How different generations create value together

The inspiration for this book is twofold: first, the observation that the current generation (Current Gen) of family business leaders remains healthy and at the helm for far longer than their predecessors; and second, the recognition that today's next generation (Next Gen) has extraordinary potential to make an immediate contribution to the family business. Traditional views of succession describe years of dutiful apprenticeship culminating in a short handover period. By contrast, recent practice shows that the Current Gen and the Next Gen can develop the business *side by side – co-evolving as peers* for a significant stretch of time. Figure 0.1 graphically describes our point of departure.

Figure 0.1 Contrasting succession and co-evolution

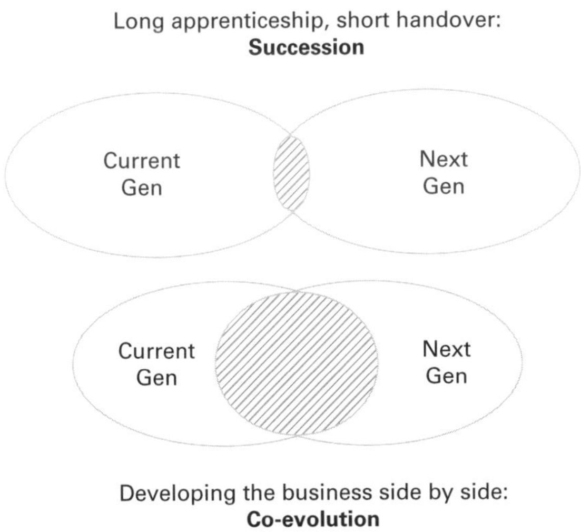

Productive co-evolution of the generations cannot be taken for granted. Highly educated and internationally experienced, the Next Gen sees a world of opportunity and wonders whether the family business is the best place to make its mark; in command for longer, the Current Gen may be tempted to put off sharing power in order to preserve what has been built. More often than not, the hierarchical nature of the parent/child relationship gets in the way of effective collaboration. A new mindset is needed. In this book, we explain how *trust maturity*, *capability appreciation* and *role respect* enable the Current Gen and Next Gen to co-evolve as peers and provide comprehensive descriptions of the *leadership practices* families employ to navigate the transition towards new ways of creating value together.

Intended for anyone connected to a family business – members of the family, non-family executives and board members, external advisers – this book breaks new ground in the study of family business by showing how to bridge the gap between the generations.[1] To do so in a manner that speaks to multiple audiences and different generations, we draw upon original company histories, fictional case studies and interdisciplinary conceptual analyses. Our aim is to motivate readers to reflect upon their own circumstances, discuss the issues they identify with members of the family and interact with the wider family business community.

Side by side in practice: Transformation initiatives

Different families find themselves on different points of a continuum from hierarchical to peer-based relations. Transformation initiatives that require young and old to work together provide some of the best illustrative material of how families can overcome hierarchical barriers between the generations.[2] While some families have been able to build on distinctive contributions from both Current and Next Gens to make important advances in strategy, sustainability and governance, others remain mired in generational disagreement. Indeed, teaming up on a transformation initiative can be a make-or-break experience. What separates the family businesses that do make the most of intergenerational collaboration from the ones that don't?

Consider the contrasting experiences of two venerable family businesses we have studied, both working in traditional sectors, undertaking for one and cheese making for the other. Pushed by the innovative drive and creative business thinking of the Next Gen and strongly supported by the Current

Gen of leadership, the Singapore-based undertakers have reconceived the very idea of memorial services, utilizing venue, sound, light and animation, to make the funeral more of a celebration of life and less of a duty of grief. As a result of this strategic transformation, the business has grown significantly and new avenues for international expansion have opened up. At the English cheese maker, on the other hand, the Next Gen has not been able to put its stamp on the business. Repeated attempts by the heirs to change the product mix or modernize the distribution system have met a wall of resistance from their elders, leaving the younger cheese makers frustrated and looking for a way out. It is particularly worth noting that neither the Singaporean nor the English transformation initiative is primarily about digitalization or even technology, where one might expect the Next Gen to put its emphasis and the Current Gen to lack understanding; both initiatives centre on traditional business strategy considerations, namely adapting the offering and delivering added value for the customer. In the first example, the generations succeeded in working together for the good of the family business; in the second example, they failed – why?

In other cases that we have studied, the opportunity for intergenerational collaboration starts not with strategy but with concerns that the Next Gen have about environmental and social sustainability.[3] Indeed, the objectives of business beyond profitability alone are one of the most frequently cited topics in discussions with the Next Gen, and generational differences in values appear more pronounced today than in the past. For a variety of reasons, broader exposure to the world, greater pressure from public interest campaigns and, in some cases, a heightened sense of guilt about privileges, today's Next Gen is more likely to express concerns about the sustainability of business than their predecessors. In this area, too, real change comes from the generations finding ways to work together to take the business forward. Thus, at an American food manufacturer, a member of the Next Gen put his misgivings about the ethics of the supply chain to the test, spending months in the field to analyse farming conditions, transportation arrangements and transfer pricing, and following up his analysis with detailed recommendations for change. In due course, his report was published on the company website, and senior management announced concrete steps to make the supply chain more transparent and fairer to all parties involved. By contrast, the attempts of a scion of a large Swiss private bank to include sustainability criteria in the firm's investments and client relationships fell on deaf ears. Her father was more than willing to consider philanthropy, but he did not want an emphasis on environmental and social sustainability to hinder his freedom of doing business. Eventually, she got paid out and co-founded an alternative asset management business that made sustainability its focus. Again, we see that the ability or the inability of the generations to work together was decisive in charting the future direction of the firm, but we don't have a ready explanation for what made the first successful and the second unsuccessful.[4]

A third type of transformation initiative that calls for the Current Gen and the Next Gen to treat each other as peers revolves around governance. Many representatives of the Next Gen are inspired by courses at university and discussions with like-minded individuals from other families to re-examine the governance of their own family business. If carried through to its logical conclusion, this process leads the Next Gen to want to initiate a governance review, or at least to ask pointed questions of the existing governance arrangements. This is exactly what happened in two cases that we are familiar with, one a ninety-year-old German regional industry leader, the other a forty-five-year-old Lebanese SME. Faced with comparable requests for information, the chair of the board and pater familias of the German firm flatly rejected the Next Gen's enquiries, while the founder of the Lebanese firm developed an appreciation for his internationally educated sons' concerns and worked together with them to carry out an extensive review of the company's governance mechanisms. How can we explain the difference in the outcomes of these two cases with comparable starting points?

Transformation initiatives centred on strategy, sustainability or governance put the Current and the Next Gens in a position to make a positive impact on the future of the family business – if they manage to work together.[5] In general, it takes time for the older and the younger to learn to treat each other as peers. Even in the 'successful' cases sketched out above, mutual understanding and fully fledged collaboration was far from immediate, with prolonged gestation periods separating the initial conversations about change from the ultimate realizations of transformation. In the cases of the English cheese maker and the Swiss private bank, on the other hand, the Next Gen experienced many years of frustration and lack of progress before accepting that collaboration with the Current Gen was not possible. As for the German regional industry leader, the chair's present rejection of the Next Gen's governance inquiry does not necessarily spell the end of the attempt at intergenerational collaboration, but it does illustrate the hierarchical distance that still needs to be overcome.

The transformation initiatives we have described are not just 'nice to have'; they are essential to the preservation of the family business. Work on strategy determines the growth and profit trajectories of the business; work on questions of sustainability affects long-term risk exposure and societal legitimacy; and work on governance sets the course for continued organizational viability as a business owned and run by the family. To the extent that today's competitive context calls for transformative efforts built around the know-how of *both* the Current and the Next Gen, then the ability of the generations to work together becomes a primary determinant of whether or not the family business adapts and remains healthy (see Figure 0.2). Of course, the Current Gen may still decide to put the Next Gen on a shelf for many years or, alternatively, to cut it loose completely, but this is done at the peril of the business. In many cases, the only economically sensible choice is for the generations to try to work together.[6]

Figure 0.2 Developing the business through transformation initiatives

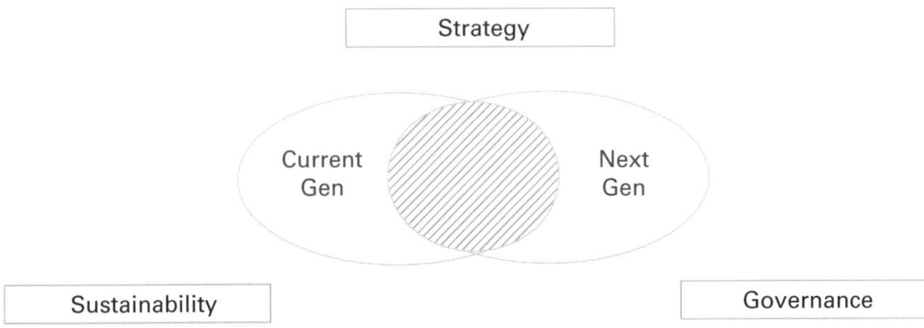

Bridging the gap between the generations

How to bridge the gap between the Current Gen and the Next Gen and facilitate peer-based co-evolution along the lines described in the successful transformation initiatives above? Recognizing the need to meet halfway is paramount. Having once been young itself, the Current Gen ought to be able to put itself in the Next Gen's shoes, or so one would think. However, the changed nature of intergenerational relationships today makes it necessary to unlearn old behaviours. In the new world that puts a premium on the ability of the generations to work together as peers, the Current Gen's hierarchical relationship with *their own* predecessors can no longer serve as a relevant model. By the same token, the Next Gen's perspective is also unique, as it impels them to assume responsibility much earlier than in the traditional hierarchical model. In sum, new behaviours are called for from both sides of the proverbial generation gap.

As we will show in this book, *trust maturity*, *capability appreciation* and *role respect* are critical enablers for the Current Gen and Next Gen to co-evolve as peers. The generations learn to trust each other's judgement, appreciate each other as capable in different domains and respect each other's distinct roles in perpetuating the business and the family. In a hierarchical relationship, the generations are likely to habitually mistrust each other's judgement, not fully appreciate their different capabilities and fail to respect the distinct roles they have to play together in ensuring the present and preparing the future of the business. In a peer-based relationship, the opposite tends to be true: more trust, greater appreciation and higher levels of respect.[7] The current reality of most family businesses lies somewhere in the middle of the scale, between the two extremes (see Figure 0.3). The path embarked upon together is what makes the difference between successful integration of the Next Gen with its entrepreneurial energy intact or alienation, staying but giving up on leaving a mark, or exiting and making a difference outside of the family business. Critically, trust maturity, capability appreciation and role respect function in a reciprocal manner; they can be represented as two-way streets. Rapprochement is possible, but so is estrangement. Making it work for the family business takes time and effort from both the Current and the Next Gens.[8]

Figure 0.3 Charting the status quo: Between peer-based and hierarchical

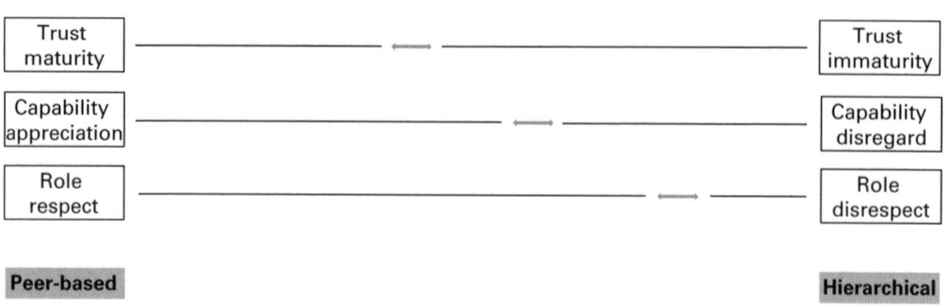

Part One – Trust maturity: Social psychology

Trust is a multi-faceted concept, critical to every human relationship, but too often it is used as an imprecise, catch-all phrase that lacks depth or contextual relevance. When *we* speak of the Current Gen and the Next Gen learning to trust each other's judgement as peers, we are not talking about the kind of implicit trust that characterizes the parent/child relationship: children trust parents to look out for their best interests and parents trust children to try their best. Instead, what we are focusing on in Part One is *trust maturity* in terms of knowing what's good for the business as a going concern and what's good for the family as a set of adult relationships, business judgement and family judgement. When trust between the generations is mature, they have confidence in each other to make the right decisions for the family business. Parents may fully trust their daughter or son, when it comes to leading their own lives, but lack trust in them when it comes to their ability to size up and make decisions for the family business. Conversely, a daughter or son may trust their parents as parents, but doubt their ability to effectively deal with all of the modern-day challenges facing the family business.

In exploring the meaning of trust maturity in Part One, we propose to do a deep dive into the social psychology of generational transition in the family business. First off, we will argue that trust maturity involves multiple levels of social interaction: communication, obligation and negotiation. Most basic for trust maturity, the Current and Next Gen break out of the parent/child relationship and build an adult relationship, that is a relationship based on the ability to communicate with each other as equal partners (Chapter 1). At a second, deeper level, Current and Next Gens move beyond the sense of obligation that permeates relationships between the generations and focus instead on enabling aspiration (Chapter 2). Finally, the conflictual intergenerational and sibling rivalries that loom behind many family business interactions yield to negotiated accord (Chapter 3). In more than a few family businesses, the sense of trust can be described with the words 'I don't trust your judgement', 'We can't talk like adults', 'I do things because I feel I have to not because I want to' and 'We fight about everything.' The goal is to transform relations so that both the Current Gen and the Next Gen can say 'I trust your judgement', 'We can talk like adults', 'I believe in what we're doing' and 'I know that when we disagree, we will find a way to move forward.'

Part Two – Capability appreciation: Strategic thinking

For the Current and the Next Gen to co-evolve as peers for the good of the family business, learning to trust each other's judgement is important, but it is not enough. As a result of their different histories, Current and Next Gens will have different capabilities, that is, different knowledge bases and different skills. For example, where the Current Gen might be particularly skilled in running the business as it is today, the Next Gen might be especially adept at developing new business models. In general, the Current Gen has more practical experience and deeper knowledge of the business; the Next Gen is likely to have more advanced academic training and broader international understanding. These differences can serve the family business, if the older and younger appreciate each other's knowledge bases and skills for what they are: not competing, but complementary. Building *capability appreciation* is the focus of Part Two.

In articulating the meaning of capability appreciation in Part Two, we will need to carefully examine the strategic thinking supporting generational transition in the family business. Capability appreciation touches multiple levels of strategic thinking. In the first place comes the classic juxtaposition of *legacy* and *change*, with the Current Gen more apt to hold on to legacy businesses and legacy methods, and the Next Gen more enthusiastic about embracing strategies for change (Chapter 4). Both generations come to understand that it is not a question of 'either/or' but rather a question of 'and'; how to combine legacy and change.

The second juxtaposition facing the generations in family business pits *practice* versus *theory* – what the Current Gen knows about business from having done it, versus what the Next Gen knows from having learned about it in school or in professional settings outside the family business and, in many cases, outside the home country (Chapter 5). Here, too, it is not a question of one being better than the other, but of recognizing and benefitting from the differences.

The third level of capability appreciation has to do with the weight accorded to *practices* from inside and outside the family business (Chapter 6). The Current Gen is more likely to see inside and outside as being in conflict, while the Next Gen has grown up with the axiom that the source of ideas is irrelevant – any idea can be useful, *taken from anywhere*, as long as it promotes innovation. Again, the point is not that one generation is wrong and the other generation is right; it's all about the two-way street of mutual appreciation.

Part Three – Role respect: Governance processes

Even where trust between the generations has matured and differing capabilities are appreciated, there may be significant conflict over roles. Typically, the Current Gen is still firmly in charge, but the Next Gen is trying to establish its position and the inherent imbalance of power can get in the way of effective collaboration. The Current Gen may seek to assert its power unnecessarily, while the Next Gen can get tangled up in unproductive battles over status. To some extent, this is an expression of the classic parent/child predicament – letting go for one, and taking over for the other. In a family business, however, these topics are more than just personal. Both generations feel a strong sense of responsibility towards the business and each may think that it alone knows what is best for the future. As a consequence, the older generation holds on to the helm for longer than it otherwise would have, while the younger generation pushes to take charge earlier. If the same people were working in a non-family company without the emotional attachment that characterizes family business, the former would probably seek retirement earlier, while the latter would not dream of taking over the reins until a lot later. *Role respect* becomes the watchword for both generations. Both the Current and the Next Gens have a specific role to play in the life of the family business – the current as a guarantor of stability, the next as a catalyst for the future (Part Three).

Role respect in family business is closely related to the development of the governance process. The more comprehensive and the better accepted the system of governance in place, the less disagreement there is likely to be about who does what when. In practice, different views of time are often a primary source of conflict over roles, with an attitude of 'wait your turn' set against an attitude of 'I'm ready now' and both generations failing to respect each other's distinct positions in the long-term evolution of the family business (Chapter 7). Instead of focusing on holding on or, conversely, taking over, the generations find ways to make the best use of the time together. Role-related questions can amplify differences between the generations over when to share power, particularly where the governance of the family business is still loosely defined or poorly implemented (Chapter 8). Family businesses that revolve around strong individual leaders and have not managed to build effective ownership committees and strong business boards feel the conflict over roles much more acutely than those that have put in place meaningful governance. Considerations of time and power, finally, come to a head around the topic of leadership succession in the family business (Chapter 9). A traditional, hierarchical perspective on succession posits the transfer of power as a very rare event, taking place once every thirty years or so; a peer-based perspective deals with succession in a more organic way, as a process that happens over time, with the involvement of multiple actors from several generations. For the Current and the Next Gens to be able to effectively work together on questions of leadership and governance requires respect – for each other's time frames, for each other's models of power sharing and for each other's distinct roles in taking the company into the future.

Each of the nine chapters outlined above leads off with a *fictional case study* that paints a concrete picture of Current Gen/Next Gen dynamics and sets the scene for the conceptual treatment to follow. Our fictional cases are based on adaptations of real life, taking slices of an anecdote from here and elements of a setting from there to illustrate the theme of the chapter. We explicitly use fiction as an active learning tool here – to bring the chapter to life in a way only fiction can and provide a basis for talking about the material, without getting into the specific background material necessary to analyse an actual company history. Readers who appreciate the evocative nature of fiction will find it particularly useful to tackle the introductory story first. If both generations of a family are reading this book, the fictional case can be a very good discussion starter – close to home in the topics it covers, but not too close. Participants in workshops and executive courses can use the fictional material to get a tangible appreciation for the ideas to be covered in the chapter and observe how the Current Gen and the Next Gen interact in a variety of true-to-life settings. To facilitate this process, we have included questions for reflection and debate at the conclusion of every fictional case study. Readers who find that fiction does not speak to them may opt to skip these fictional cases and focus on the fictional case and *conceptual approach*, a more conventional treatment of the theme being studied that emphasizes the results of academic inquiry and speaks to practical experience. The conceptual approach to the chapter builds on established thinking in family business to establish a base, but then adds another layer of reflection, bringing to bear insights and fresh thinking from the disciplines of social psychology, strategy/economics and governance/political science. In this manner, readers are encouraged to look at the age-old question of collaboration between the generations in new ways. Each of the first nine chapters concludes with a workbook consisting of a set of questions about the conceptual approach, for discussion within the generations and between the generations, as well as suggestions for workshops and executive courses. The idea is to use the reading as a launch pad for thinking about and, critically, discussing how the family of the readers approaches trust maturity, capability appreciation and role respect.

Part Four – Navigating the transition: Action

To offer a better understanding of what it takes to *support the shift* from hierarchical to peer-based relations between the generations and from succession to co-evolution as a model for family business, we complement the analyses of trust maturity, capability appreciation and role respect presented in Parts One, Two and Three with descriptions of *leadership practices* that families put to use in the transition process (Part Four). Whereas the first three parts of the book make use of fictional cases to initiate discussion, the fourth part draws on the lessons from original company histories to provide baselines to work with in implementing the side-by-side approach to generational transition in practice. Baselines are not recipes, and taking action is never a simple matter of adopting the experience of others. As Tolstoy pointed out in the first sentence of *Anna Karenina*, 'Happy families are all alike; every unhappy family is unhappy in its own way.' In other words, every family is unique and no general rules can be expected to apply across the board, without significant adaptation. It is in the spirit of suggesting possible ways forward, then, that we share the practical experiences of the business families we have worked with and studied.

Taken as a set, these families' experiences indicate that treating generational transition as a journey means employing distinctive leadership practices that work over time, in different doses and in different ways, as the transition progresses. It is not a question of 'If at stage x, then do y'; instead, families work with leadership practices that can be applied across stages and regulate how the generations interact. What we observe in the field is the pairing of a leadership practice that promotes the individual and aspirational with a leadership practice that upholds the collective and foundational, creating a dynamic tension between allowing individuals to maximize their potential and getting the basics right to ensure collective standards (Chapter 10). Since transformation initiatives can play a critical role in establishing peer-to-peer collaboration between the generations, we also want to offer some practical guidance on how to run them. Accordingly, we present a number of examples, covering the launch of a transformation initiative, the process of building momentum over the course of a transformation initiative, the practice of embedding a transformation initiative in the organization and the act of bringing a transformation initiative to its natural conclusion (Chapter 11). Each family business faces its own particular context and works out its own path. This book is intended as a resource for family businesses, describing what can be done and what has been done, rather than what should be done. We aim to help readers find what they need, develop techniques to talk about it and share what works for them with a broader community. To support self-learning, moderated workshop learning and classroom learning for families and students of family business, we provide advice based on our teaching and consulting experience and show how to use the different pedagogical tools described in this book (Chapter 12). In the Epilogue, finally, we reflect upon the broader implications of a side-by-side mindset, for the family business and beyond.

Past, present and future of family business

Fundamentally, the themes of this book find echoes in classical and literary texts on families. The conflict between father and son over the fitness to lead and the timing to take over, for example, is already a foundational topic in Greek mythology. Tales of sons prematurely trying to take over from their fathers also feature in the Bible, while Shakespeare's *King Lear* dramatizes the daughters' betrayal of their father. The founder of modern psychology, Sigmund Freud, goes so far as to base his entire theory of the human subconscious upon the father/son rivalry, drawing his own inspiration from the ancient Greek story of Oedipus. The moral opposite of the father/son conflict, namely a son's obligation to respect and obey his father, also has significant classical antecedents. Thus, filial respect serves as a cornerstone of traditions as diverse as Confucianism and Roman ethics and is stressed as an imperative by most of today's major religions. In summary, the question of how the generations interact is age-old and mythology, literature and religion offer memorable descriptions and valuable explanations. The same holds true for the findings of modern sociology and social psychology, as they concern the family and shed light on the relationships between parents and adult children. Where appropriate, therefore, we will draw on insights from the classics and the social sciences. While acknowledging our intellectual forebears, however, we also want to try to break new ground: rather than succession, forced or natural, our focus is on how the generations can co-evolve; rather than parental duty and filial piety, both hierarchical relationships, our concern is with how the generations can work together side by side as peers.

Although the family and the parent/child relationship have always been and still are central to cultural norms (and narratives) the world over, significant differences of emphasis can be observed. Family businesses themselves, in turn, are more diverse in terms of leadership and governance than listed companies, free as they are from the normalizing constraints imposed by stock exchanges and international shareholders. In other words, the global landscape of family business is nothing if not varied. Nonetheless, our approach to understanding intergenerational collaboration in family business is universalistic and we draw upon a pool of examples from around the world. There are two principal reasons for this choice. First, members of the Next Gen are increasingly similar to each other, no matter where the home base of the family business is. They study at the same American and British universities, most of them consume similar products, cultural and otherwise, and all of them are subject to the levelling influences of social media. What's more, and as we will describe in more detail below, the Next Gen is very active in sharing experiences with each other across family businesses from different geographies. All of this has a standardizing effect, reducing, if not eliminating, cultural specificities. Our second reason for preferring a universalistic approach builds on the first but has more to do with the institution of the family business than the individual family members. Most family businesses of a certain size actively compare their experiences with those of other family businesses, in their home country, but also abroad. Thus, although family businesses, unlike listed companies, do not *have* to follow the same rules, they actively seek to learn from each other either in direct discussions among families (owner to owner) or mediated by university leadership programmes for families and international consultants. This leads to the widespread adoption of similar best practices and weakens cultural specificity. Of course, cultural differences do not disappear altogether, and they remain relevant to how individual family members perceive themselves and to how family businesses act. Therefore, even though we choose to adopt a universalistic approach to theorizing about and offering suggestions to family business, we remain sensitive to deep-seated cultural specificities and point these out wherever they may be critical.

Preserving and growing the family business

A guiding assumption for our work is that preserving and growing the family business is a desirable outcome. Without getting into the intricacies of the argument for and against inheritance laws, suffice it to say that we view ownership and a fortiori ownership of a business as both a right and a responsibility.[9] We further assume that some, if not all, members of the Next Gen are interested in making their own contributions to the development of the family business.[10] In formulating any specific plans based on our work, it is important to bear real-life constraints in mind, in terms of both human resources and organizational resources. In family business, especially, the capabilities and aspirations of the individual protagonists have to be taken into consideration: what skills do the different generations possess and how does each want to contribute to the business? Although side by side may be a generally desirable outcome for the future of the family business, one-size-fits-all definitely does not apply and families need to work with what they have. Similarly, at the organizational level, resource-rich businesses with a secure competitive advantage will have more room to experiment with the concepts presented here than resource-poor businesses that need to transform quickly. Ultimately, what matters is how the Current and Next Gens make sense of the circumstances, for themselves and for the family business.

There can be situations in which selling and starting over is a better path forward, for the business and for the family. The business may flourish under a different owner and the family may revive without the business. Even then, however, our experience indicates that peer-based relations between the Current and the Next Gens offer a more stable basis for a smooth transition to a new status quo than decisions made by decree. Looking beyond the concerns of today and tomorrow, both the Current and the Next Gen may want to bear in mind that they are under observation. Still children or adolescents, the next Next Gen is watching and listening. How they see and hear the generations ahead of them interacting will undoubtedly have an effect on their desire to one day participate in the family business. Peer-based relations built on mutual understanding are a better advertisement for the family business than hierarchical clashes.[11]

The transition from hierarchical to peer-based relations between the generations in family business is a journey that may take a considerable amount of time. Both the Current Gen and the Next Gen are called upon to adapt. This book breaks the journey down into its constitutive parts and shows how the generations can learn to trust, appreciate and respect each other as peers. Each family business has a unique starting point and each family business has its own capacity for change. Each family will take a different path. More often than not, change in the family business comes from within, driven by both generations' sense of purpose and long-term orientation. We think family businesses are capable of transforming themselves on their own. If this book can function as a reference for family businesses that are looking for guidance and inspiration in making the generational transition, our purpose in writing it will have been well served.

PART ONE
Trust maturity
Social psychology

Your children are not your children.
They are sons and daughters of Life's longing for itself.
They come through you but not from you.
And though they are with you yet they belong not to you.
You may give them your love but not your thoughts,
For they have their own thoughts.
You may house their bodies but not their souls,
For their souls dwell in the house of tomorrow, which you cannot visit, not even in your dreams.
You may strive to be like them, but seek not to make them like you.
For life goes not backward nor tarries with yesterday.
You are the bows from which your children as living arrows are sent forth.
The archer sees the mark upon the path of the infinite and He bends you with His might that His arrows may go swift and far.
Let your bending in the archer's hand be for gladness.
For even as He loves the arrow that flies, so He also loves the bow that is stable.

KAHLIL GIBRAN, 'ON CHILDREN', *THE PROPHET* (1923)

This poem stands for many similar efforts to capture the difficulty of communicating and the gap of understanding between young and old, children and parents, or, in our context, the Next Gen and the Current Gen. Perhaps the best-known treatment of this classic theme in modern popular culture is Cat Stevens' iconic song, 'Father and son', a ballad about youthful rebellion in the face of parental conservatism.[1] Incompatible ways of communicating and different visions of the future standing in the way of deeper trust – it's a familiar story to every family business and indeed to all adult children and all parents of adult children. How to go beyond endlessly replaying the parts assigned by the deeply ingrained patterns of parent/child relationships? How to build reciprocal trust between the Current Gen and the Next Gen? These are the questions we propose to address in Part One of the book, focusing on the relationship(s) between the generations and drawing upon insights from social psychology.

Trust is a multi-faceted and much misused concept and trust between the generations of a family business is a subject in and of itself. When we speak of the Current Gen and the Next Gen learning to trust each other's judgement as peers, we are not talking about the kind of implicit trust that characterizes the parent/child relationship. Instead, what we are focusing on in Part One is *trust maturity* in terms of knowing what's good for the business as a going concern and what's good for the family as a set of adult relationships, business judgement and family judgement. When trust between the generations is mature, they have confidence in each other to make the right decisions for the family business. Trust maturity involves multiple levels of social interaction. Most fundamentally, the Current and Next Gen break out of the parent/child relationship and build an adult relationship, that is a relationship based on the ability to communicate with each other as equal partners (Chapter 1). At a second, deeper level, both the Current and Next Gens move beyond the sense of obligation that permeates relationships between the generations and focus instead on enabling aspiration – I want to, rather than I have to (Chapter 2). Finally, the conflictual intergenerational and sibling rivalries that loom behind many family business interactions yield to negotiated accord (Chapter 3).

Learning approach: Side by side as social psychology

Many of the most influential texts in the relatively young field of family business are based on family psychology, the psychology of individuals and groups as it is shaped by the context of growing up and living in a family.[2] While we incorporate insights from these foundational works, our focus in Part One of this book is different: not on a psychological characterization of relationships in the family, but on a detailed examination of the dynamics of intergenerational relationships. We want to know how intergenerational relationships evolve and how these relationships in turn affect collaboration in the family business. For this purpose, we draw liberally on the analytical tools of social psychology, the broad area of study devoted to describing and explaining how people interact. The ultimate objective, in this part of the book, is to shine the spotlight on the mechanisms that enable the formation of trust maturity between the Current and the Next Gen of family business leaders.

- **Point of departure**

  → *The social psychology of intergenerational relationships is critical to succession.* Whereas family psychology has received a lot of attention in the study of family business, the broader field of social psychology has not been fully exploited in efforts to describe and explain relationships in family businesses. Essentially, succession is about the evolution of intergenerational relationships. As such, the theory and practice of succession in family business both stand to gain from the incorporation of the broader set of insights available in social psychology. In particular, building upon a social psychology perspective suggests that relationships can be worked upon and changed, that even family relationships are not doomed to remain stuck in established or even archetypal patterns. In other words, studying the social psychology of intergenerational relationships may yield actionable implications, results that families can make use of in developing their own approach to succession.

- **Important assumptions**

  → *Inclusive, fair exchange is necessary for sustaining the family business of today.* Which is better, dominant top-down decision-making, or inclusive, fair exchange that draws on a variety of relevant inputs? The debate is as old as the study of business and there is no easy answer. It all depends on the situation and on the people. In the context of many of today's family businesses, there are two important reasons to think that inclusive, fair exchange is particularly relevant. First of all, a more complex business environment – the heightened impact of new technologies and the bigger diversity of competitive threats – requires more broad-based input into decision-making. Simply put and as information processing theory would predict, greater uncertainty demands more and better information.[3] Over and above the changing nature of the business environment, family businesses have to consider the changing nature of the family and, especially, the new opportunities available to the Next Gen. The Next Gen does not *have* to work in the family business; compared to the past, opportunities for them are much more varied. Hence, it is necessary to get their buy-in, both to contributing their energies to the family business and to supporting the decisions made, and inclusive, fair exchange is better suited to gaining their commitment than dominant, top-down decision-making.

- **Normative implications**

  → *Families build a decision-making culture that gives voice to multiple generations.* It is possible for business families to build a decision-making culture that gives voice to multiple generations: it can be done, we have seen it done. In some cases, it appears to happen naturally, almost given from the start, based on the way the founder wants (wanted) it to be or just on how the family works. In other cases, it takes a lot of hard work, even years of effort, to change the decision-making culture from dominant and hierarchical to inclusive and based not on seniority but on merit. The three chapters presented in Part One are aimed at building an understanding for what it takes and establishing the basis for both self-reflection and discussion in the family. Part Four offers examples of what business families have actually done to build a decision-making culture that gives voice to multiple generations without becoming an unruly cacophony.

From parent/ child to adult peers

01

Level conversations

CASE STUDY

Fictional case 1

Young Grace took 'study' trips to Florence and traded in a one-year-old Maserati for a new Ferrari; her father Henry made the rounds of his refineries on the Malacca Strait in a 1993 Mercedes 280E. She was into art history and fashion; he liked nothing more than catching up with old school friends in a coffee shop.

Unmarried, Grace still lived in her parents' home and, unless overseas travel kept father and daughter apart, they never went more than a day without talking. In general, Grace did not so much consult with her father about life as tell him what she was doing in her day to day: shopping, restaurants and parties. One morning, on his way out the door, she surprised him with a novel request.

'I want to start a business and I need you to help me!'

'A business? Now that's something new – what kind of business?'

'I'm thinking of a line of tops for women, something so special and so hard to find that everybody who is anybody will be dying to have one!'

'Tops – you mean blouses?'

'Yes! Blouses, shirts, Ts, tank tops, halters. I'll be needing some seed money.'

'How much seed money exactly?'

'Oh, I don't know, one million, maybe two to start with?'

'That's a lot of money.'

'Not more than you would be giving me for an apartment in Paris or London.'

'I don't know. Starting a business is not the same thing as buying an apartment. I'll have to think about it.'

When she met her two best friends for drinks later that same day, Grace hadn't yet got over the shock of her father's reluctance to write her a blank cheque.

'I don't understand it. He never refuses me anything. It can't be the money. We're not talking about a lot here, just a basis for starting out, nothing really.'

'When it's about bags or trips or cars, they never care,' said her friend Nancy, 'but when it comes to business, they think they know it all.'

'You have to learn to speak his language, market positioning, cost of capital, internal rate of return, that kind of thing,' continued Nancy.

Grace had been around the oil business all her life, or rather the oil business had been all around her, but her understanding of how to make money did not run deep. The basic notions – supply and demand, buying low and selling high – were familiar from having heard them floating around family dinners from as early as she could remember. Beyond that, and the potential to tap her father's cash and his web of relations, the one business skill she could be sure of was her ability to nose out trends: whatever new fashion Grace picked up on for herself, be it in makeup, in accessories, in clothes, or even in restaurants or vacation spots seemed to eventually become a must-have, not only among her friends, but also in the wider community of young luxury aficionados around her. Recently, maybe over the last year or so, she had begun to dream about turning that special flair of hers for getting ahead of the game into something more. She knew that people saw her as a 'daddy's girl'. Launching a successful business in her own right, in a field as far away as possible from oil, would establish her as someone to be reckoned with – Grace first, Henry's daughter second.

Nancy's comment about speaking the language of business brought Grace back down to earth. It wouldn't be as simple as she had imagined, there was still a long way to go. Where to start? Grace knew a lot of people, but she wasn't used to asking for help. In her circle of friends, young women and men who like herself had grown up in the shadow of successful business founders, there were several who had gone the start-up route and might be called upon to share their expertise with her. She settled on the most inconspicuous of the bunch, Andy. He was pleased to be invited to contribute and immediately set out to organize Grace's vague collection of ideas into a coherent business plan. Where she was intuitive, he was systematic; where she trusted her gut feel, he relied on figures. They fine-tuned the business model over the following few months; his meticulousness exasperated her as much as her impulsiveness annoyed him, but they stuck with it. Together, they hit on the name 'Talisman Tops' and presented the label to focus groups in several cities across Southeast Asia. Once marketing plans had been outlined and product requirements established, it wasn't that hard to estimate potential sales and think through production and distribution arrangements – always with Andy's technical help, but grounded in Grace's distinct vision: 'something so special and so hard to find that everybody who is anybody will be dying to have one'.

For his part, the oil baron decided to learn about the fashion business. If he was going to make an investment, he needed to understand the ins-and-outs. Oil was about managing scarcity and controlling distribution, 'putting on the squeeze', as he called it. From a distance, fashion, particularly high-end fashion, looked like a very different animal: convincing people who already had everything to buy even more at a price that had no relation to the cost of production. Even though it didn't make any sense to him, there was a billion-dollar market for this kind of thing and, what's more, this market required a lot less investment in fixed assets than he was used to with oil; it seemed to be all about image.

To get a better feel for what made the high-end fashion market tick, Henry contacted some local business friends who had interests in textiles. They were more than happy to talk, but also quick to admit that they had no idea how luxury worked. The profitability and the mystique of the big brands were a mystery to them. All they really knew was that the share prices of the big fashion conglomerates were on a multi-year tear. Henry ought to go straight to the source, they advised: Paris and Milan.

A firm believer in the power of entrepreneurs, Grace's father scoured the internet for information on the backgrounds and careers of Bernard Arnault and François Pinault, the French moguls who between them controlled well over half of the world's luxury brands. Armed with this knowledge, he arranged to speak to the Goldman Sachs sell-side analyst covering the firms of the two men. Marvelling at the history of growth by acquisition and appreciating the financials of Arnault's LVMH and Pinault's Kering, Henry found himself starting to take a real interest in the business of luxury. He even spent an afternoon wandering around incognito at The Starhill luxury shopping mall, to get a first-hand impression of what drove women and some men to spend so much money on the big names.

At length, he made up his mind: Grace should get some experience in one of the two major houses, ideally at the side of one of their top marketers. Accordingly, he stretched out his feelers and put his contacts to work.

Andy had advised Grace that it would be better – it would look that much more professional – if she made an appointment with her father to discuss the business plan for Talisman Tops with him. When the big day came, she was well prepared, plan in hand, numbers and arguments at her fingertips. Henry was also ready: he had just reached an understanding with the Asia Head of LVMH. Grace would be spending the next six months at the company's headquarters on Avenue Montaigne in Paris.

The conceptual approach

The parent/child relationship is the mother of all hierarchical relationships. As children grow older, the original differences in strength and knowledge diminish and the relationship evolves. Nonetheless, something of the parent/child gradient always remains, even after the children become adults. In a family business, parents and children may work together as adults, but many parents still see their children first as children and many adult children still see their parents first as parents. This inherently hierarchical mindset prevents parents and children from accepting each other as peers and gets in the way of effective intergenerational collaboration. Parent/child thinking plays into all aspects of working together in the family business: communications, expectations and decision-making processes. We will cover each of these topics in turn, but in Chapter 1 we start with communication as the most basic building block. Having *adult conversations* is fundamental to establishing trust maturity.

Analysing conversations in the family

What is an adult conversation? In the context of a business, the expression 'adult conversation' would, at first glance, seem out of place. Aren't shareholders, board members, executives, middle managers and frontline employees all adults who relate to each other as adults, and not as adults and children? It is worth recalling that, in this respect at least, family businesses have a long record of being different. Throughout the 19th century and until deep into the 20th century in some cases and in some countries, it was common to look at the man (or, much more rarely, the woman) at the head of the family business as the father figure not only of his blood descendants but also of the larger family of employees. Hence the common use of the word 'patron' in France, leader and father.[1] A father does not treat his children as adults, but as dependents that he has the responsibility to care for, in good times and bad times.

Although the old-style patron does not hold sway anymore, today's family businesses still maintain some traces of the old system, particularly where family members are concerned. In many families, and this is the case across cultures, it is understood that the Current Gen takes care of the Next Gen. Although laudable in and of itself, taking care also implies planning ahead and setting guidelines, in effect acting as a parent for children long after the latter have reached adulthood. Parental behaviour naturally expresses itself in conversations between the generations. Even if the Current and the Next Gen are talking about a decision which is strictly business, i.e. an investment in a new technology or a new business, the conversation is likely not to be the same as the conversation that a family CEO would have with a non-family executive about the same subject. With the non-family executive, the family CEO will talk strictly business: expected margins, required resources, unforeseen eventualities, etc. The family CEO will not be talking about or even thinking about parental feelings and today's non-family executive will certainly not be acting the part of the child. In an adult conversation, the counterparties are not parent and child, but rather independent individuals who are able to treat each other as peers and focus on the subject at hand. When different generations of a family are involved, by contrast, the same conversation may take on a whole different character, with the parent/child relationship overshadowing or at least strongly influencing everything else.

Before discussing how to have an adult conversation in a family business setting, it is useful to think about the barriers to an adult conversation between the generations. Academic research in the field of human communication is extraordinarily rich and varied, with linguists, social scientists of all stripes and philosophers each proposing their own models. Although no one model has primacy, notions of power, emotional attachment and persistence of patterns over time are seen as common threads, particularly where conversation among family members is concerned.[2] On the one hand, differences in the relative status of family members, both across and within generations, are reflected in everyday interactions, with even benign exchanges providing occasions to reinforce existing power gradients: how people address each other, who speaks first/who speaks last, respective use of tone and volume, etc. On the other hand, every interaction in the family is also an expression of relative emotional connection: affection or disaffection/dislike, close feelings for each other, or indifference, dependence or independence, etc. Not only are status differences and emotional attachments ever-present in family conversations, these characteristics, are also embedded in very long shared histories, and these histories have established patterns of relating to each other that can seem set in stone, leading to seemingly endless loops of repetition in which old subjects are brought up again and again, and old ways of behaving with each other resurface whenever there is tension or disagreement. All this to say that it is very hard to have a level, objective and creatively productive conversation in the family: family conversations tend to reflect differences in status and varying degrees of emotional connectedness, while repeating long-established patterns in terms of what is said and how it is said.

Enabling adult conversations

At its most basic, an adult conversation between the Current Gen and the Next Gen takes place on a playing field where parent/child status differences are acknowledged and then put aside, positive and negative emotions are held in check and deep-rooted habits of interaction are actively questioned. In the abstract, that is a very tall order. In effect, the Current Gen and the Next Gen are asked to become experts at analysing their own conversations, like a third person in the room, observing their own behaviours and adjusting on the fly, when the parent/child pattern of conversation threatens to take over. Unsurprisingly, many conversations between the Current Gen and the Next Gen fail to live up to this standard. Often enough, and as theory would predict, the generations fall back into the well-worn groove of past conversations (i.e. pushing each other's buttons or recalling past failures) and end up frustrated by the difficulty of finding common ground. It is easy to think to yourself or even say out loud, 'Let's have an adult conversation'; it is much more challenging in practice, particularly when difficult questions about the business and the family are on the table.

Families who have made the effort to engage in adult-type conversations early on, i.e. from adolescence, may have an easier time. Thus, as multiple guides to the practice of family business advise, it is definitely helpful to educate adolescents and young adults in the basics of the business, showing them around the office or factory, introducing them to key non-family employees and organizing events that bring the business to life for them.

Pursued over a number of years, this process builds interest in the business and gives the Next Gen the rudiments of a vocabulary to work with. Furthermore, if their input is already solicited at an early age, it can give them the confidence that they will be taken seriously. However, even families that engage in the effort to bring the Next Gen along from an early age cannot assume that adult conversations will be the norm. The psychological barriers discussed above, status differences, emotional ties and frustrating patterns or habits of long standing are too high to be overcome by sporadic business introduction events alone. In other words, even families that teach their kids to talk business need substantive reinforcement.

Awareness is undoubtedly the first step. Are members of the Current Gen aware of the hierarchical, parent/child effect they are having on the conversation, each time they:

- assume the attitude of a benefactor;
- resort to a father/mother knows best explanation; or
- play the guilt card, asking for appreciation from the Next Gen?

Conversely, are the Next Gen aware of the hierarchical, parent/child effect they are having on the conversation, each time they:

- assume the attitude of a supplicant;
- accept a father/mother knows best explanation; or
- object to the guilt card, but continue in a pattern of mutual accusation?

We should emphasize that these are only a few of the traps that conversations between Current Gens and Next Gens can fall into. There are many others, and they all have something to do with how the generations play their roles as parents and children, traditionally hierarchical or unconventionally as peers. As discussed, awareness of how the parent/child pattern appears is the first step in recognizing and persisting in adult conversations. Unfortunately, awareness alone is not enough. The problem is that it is too easy to revert to the parent/child types of conversation that have characterized the relationship since childhood, even if both generations have their respective radars up and promise each other and themselves to make every effort to do things differently. The context and structure of the conversation also need to be carefully considered.

Setting up conversations to succeed

How to set up an adult conversation so that it does not degenerate into a parent/child conversation? Conversations can be analysed in a multitude of ways, but here topic, format and process are the most relevant. There is a better chance for having an adult conversation if the topic is *well defined* rather than mixed or muddled, and if the issue to be discussed requires *substantial input from both generations* rather than depending only on one or the other. A well-defined topic, such as an investment decision, sets the stage for an adult conversation far better than a motley collection of topics: the former implies a clear agenda, while the latter allows the parties to the conversation to equivocate and often ends up with an airing of grievances that hearkens back to past conversations and doesn't resolve anything. Moreover, if one side or the other is in a position of having less experience with the subject under consideration, often, but not always, this would be the Next Gen, then there is an increased probability of hierarchical behaviour, even if the topic is well defined. The phrases 'You don't understand this well enough' and 'Come back and talk to me after you have done your homework' represent typical and not-so-subtle reminders about who is in charge. Especially when families are just learning how to have adult conversations, it is important to work with topics that can only be resolved by both generations listening to each other and drawing upon each other for complementary insights.

Adult conversation is further encouraged by the right type of format. At a minimum, a specific time is put aside for serious discussion, rather than trying to address a topic which is important to the family business in passing or on the run, as so often happens in business families. Having a specific time and place, with a list of required participants, makes everybody conscious of the significance of the conversation and reduces the likelihood that people will take the easy way out of asserting hierarchical positions or treating the discussion in a condescending manner that avoids the issue at hand. Of course, much of the interaction between the generations is informal, but, at least for topics related to the business or the family as the caretaker of the business, every effort should be made to define not only the topic but also the format of the discussion.

However carefully chosen the topic and the format, it still comes down to process. Questions of tone, vocabulary, talk time and attitude are primordial. Both the Current Gen and the Next Gen are asked to question themselves: is my tone authoritarian or tolerant? An authoritarian, dominant tone of voice suggests 'I know better' and establishes a pecking order; a tolerant tone, on the other hand, involves more listening and signals openness to different ideas, whatever their source. Do I use words or phrases that imply superiority or do I look for ways to express myself without an inbuilt claim to leadership? References to one's own expertise and experience are generally not conducive to a productive exchange of opinions. Do we manage to roughly balance talk time and listen time, or is one side taking over? Both the Current Gen and the Next Gen can be guilty of hijacking the conversation and a lecture rarely convinces the other side. Most importantly, perhaps, are we avoiding being judgemental of the person in front of us and trying our best to stay analytical about the issue? Judgements based on a shared history are an inevitable feature of conversations in families and family businesses: 'You were always a dreamer' or 'You were always the lazy one.' The challenge in building the right atmosphere for adult conversations is to put these judgements aside, or, when they do rear their heads, as they will, call them out for what they are: harmful preconceptions that get in the way of the generations finding common ground and working together effectively.

Going beyond conversations

Adult conversations don't just happen. It takes a lot of goodwill from all concerned and plenty of practice. Despite having the right topic and format in place and paying painstaking attention to getting the process right, conversations between the generations can still derail and fall back into well-worn patterns of parent/child dependence, leading to the unearthing old grievances and culminating in mutual accusations. In dealing with such breakdowns, it is important to recognize that the ever-present parent/child dynamic only represents one possible cause; expectations of loyalty and feelings of obligation (see Chapter 2), as well as conflicts over power and rivalries between and within the generations (see Chapter 3), also play an important role in encouraging or, more commonly, getting in the way of adult conversations. The conversation as such is often only the tip of the iceberg, and the signs of things going bad may be subtle and hard to pinpoint. Not everything will be said. Thus, having an adult conversation along the lines described here is an ideal worth striving for, and a building block to stronger intergenerational collaboration, but cannot be an end in itself. In other words, even if not all of a family's conversations meet the 'adult standard' – and they won't – efforts from both generations to build bridges cannot stop here. As we will show in the succeeding chapters, the ability to have adult conversations depends in no small measure on resetting expectations in the family and addressing conflictual rivalries.

As many volumes of research have shown, family conversations tend to reflect differences in status and varying degrees of emotional connectedness while repeating long-established patterns in terms of what is said and how it is said. No matter how strong the desire to do things differently, on the part of one generation or the other or both, these barriers to adult conversation remain very difficult to overcome. In a conversation involving parents and their offspring, or uncles/aunts and their nephews/nieces, hierarchy and everything that comes with it is ever-present and cannot be wished away. The best chance for adult conversation is to acknowledge the influence of hierarchy and the barriers to communication inherent in the parent/child relationship and address them.

KEY TAKEAWAYS

1. Parent/child behaviour patterns are barriers to adult conversations in the family business.
2. Adult conversations between the generations require focused effort and practice.
3. Adult conversation is the essential starting point for side-by-side development of the family business.

Learning journey: Pit stop 1

Please refer to Chapter 12 for a full explanation of the educational approach supporting the learning journey.

SELF-LEARNING

Self-assessment

Assess where the Current Gen and the Next Gen in your family business are and should be on the continuum between parent/child and adult conversations.

Self-reflection

Current Gen: Think through the following statements. How true are they of your own situation?

I know how to talk with members of the Next Gen: I understand them.

When I talk with the Next Gen, it's from one adult to another.

I keep parent/child patterns out of conversations with the Next Gen.

Next Gen: Think through the following statements – how true are they of your own situation?

I know how to talk with members of the Current Gen: I understand them.

When I talk with the Current Gen, it's from one adult to another.

I keep parent/child patterns out of conversations with the Current Gen.

Development plan for Current Gen/Next Gen

Draw up a development plan in which you define the following milestones:

Short term: What will I do by next week to close the conversation gap? What will I consider a success by then?

Mid-term: What will I do by next month to close the conversation gap? What will I consider a success by then?

Long term: What will I do by next year to close the conversation gap? What will I consider a success by then?

Action review

Mark the dates in your calendar when you check how well you have achieved the short-, medium- and long-term goals you set. Evaluate what you have achieved and look back at what went well and what went poorly.

MODERATED WORKSHOP LEARNING

Group discussion

Use the material presented in Chapter 1 as a launch pad for thinking about and critically discussing how the family approaches conversations.

For the Current Gen, first prepare yourself, then discuss with the Next Gen:

When do conversations with the Next Gen about the family business (i.e. topics, settings) go especially well?

When do they go poorly?

For the Next Gen, first prepare yourself, then discuss with the Current Gen:

When do conversations with the Current Gen about the family business (i.e. topics, settings) go especially well?

When do they go poorly?

Case discussion

Read fictional case 1 and discuss the following questions:

Put yourself in the position of Grace: how should Grace react to Henry's offer to arrange an internship at LVMH?

Put yourself in the position of Henry: how should Henry react to the business plan Grace will present to him?

As a consultant to the family, how would you advise Grace and Henry to raise the level of their communications?

Case simulation

Replay the conversation between Grace and her father in your own words.

For the Next Gen, assume the role of Grace's father.

For the Current Gen, assume the role of Grace.

Starting positions: Grace reacts to Henry's offer of an LVMH internship; Henry reacts to Grace's business plan.

Those who are not involved in the simulation observe and comment.

Development plan for Current Gen/Next Gen

Draw up a development plan in which you define the following milestones:

Short term: What will I do by next week to close the conversation gap? What will I consider a success by then?

Medium term: What will I do by next month to close the conversation gap? What will I consider a success by then?

Long term: What will I do by next year to close the conversation gap? What will I consider a success by then?

Co-coaching

Choose a partner from a different generation and share your development plan with him or her. Arrange two follow-up meetings after two months and after six months to see how well you have implemented your plan.

CLASSROOM LEARNING

Group discussion

Use the material presented in Chapter 1 as a launch pad for thinking about and critically discussing how families approach conversations.

When do conversations between the Current and Next Gen about the family business go especially well?

When do they go poorly?

Case discussion

Read fictional case 1 and discuss the following questions:

> *Put yourself in the position of Grace: how should Grace react to Henry's offer to arrange an internship at LVMH?*
>
> *Put yourself in the position of Henry: how should Henry react to the business plan Grace will present to him?*
>
> *As a consultant to the family, how would you advise Grace and Henry to raise the level of their communications?*

Case simulation

Replay the conversation between Grace and her father in your own words.

Starting positions: Grace reacts to Henry's offer of an LVMH internship; Henry reacts to Grace's business plan.

Those who are not involved in the simulation observe and comment.

Oxford-style debate

Form two teams and prepare to debate the following thesis, with one team in favour and the other team against:

> It is the job of the Current Gen to create the conditions that allow for a peer-to-peer conversation between the Current Gen and the Next Gen.

Conduct a debate to collect all possible and valid arguments for and against the proposal.

Case report

Choose a family business that you know or are familiar with, and analyse how the conversations between the Current and Next Gen are going and how they have evolved over time. Make concrete suggestions on how the conversations could be further improved to make them truly peer-to-peer.

From obligation to aspiration 02

Reset expectations

CASE STUDY

Fictional case 2

'You don't have to… of course not… but I think… it would be good… for your own growth.'

Is this going to be a typical father/daughter story, the kind experienced by so many Next Gens working with and for their founder parents? You can picture the characters: he, a highly accomplished self-made businessman, active in a variety of fields, extremely sure of himself; she, the youngish, well-meaning heiress, with interests from art to philanthropy, not always confident in her own abilities. Where he prepares and dresses with an informality that emphasizes his life of success, she changes looks and outfits with her moods. He trusts her completely as far as character goes and plans to groom her to become his successor; she feels indebted to him, but isn't sure whether or not she can handle the businesses he wants to put in her care. The exchange could be taking place in Asia, in the Middle East, or in Europe, it doesn't really matter where: cultures and religions differ, but parent/child relations are universal.

'I think it would be good for your own growth.' How often had she heard that ambivalent line from him.

At first, she would turn him down – too busy right now, too many things on her plate. After all, she had her own life to live.

Insist he never did, just a raised eyebrow here or a sad smile there, to let her know that he was still thinking about it.

Eventually – every time – the guilt got to her and she gave in. It was only going to be for a short while, she told herself, just a blip in the electrocardiogram of her career.

She attacked each new assignment from him as if it were her last: whether reviewing the books of an errant subsidiary, reorganizing the human resource function at head office, or taking charge of a freshly acquired business, it didn't matter, she ran with whatever he threw at her.

There it is again, that desire to impress. Why? A carryover from childhood, no doubt, a need for affirmation, not a rational choice. Instead of a 9-to-5 mentality, it's a full-time commitment. If the family calls, it's different. No questions asked, do what it takes: one month, six months, one year. After all, the family business belongs to the family, so it's everyone's responsibility to help when needed.

The first week or so, he would leave her to her own devices. Then, the calls would start to come in – early in the morning, or late at night, whenever he felt the urge. Had she thought of this? Had she looked at that? What about consulting Mr X, or asking advice from Mrs Y?

She had the job, but, behind the scenes, he was in charge. Invariably, he would take it upon himself to talk with a key employee, redesign a difficult job or make a critical hire. Call it second-guessing, if you like. It was his way of helping out.

For him, it's never meddling, it's always loving and caring. What's wrong with benefitting from experience? Of course, young people have to make their own mistakes, that's the only way they'll learn, but the right word of advice here or the timely personal connection there can save everybody a lot of trouble – and a lot of money. The family gets whatever help they need, that's the rule. For the Current Gen, it's personal. The Next Gen ought to appreciate the support. Can't let family fail, that just wouldn't do.

There would be the predictable blow up, followed by the predictable reconciliation.

She knew where it would lead. Why should this time be any different from previous times?

Taking a step back, it sounds like a song on endless repeat. Each time is different, each time is the same. Best intentions, eyes wide open, but then things happen and reality takes over. Maybe some people just aren't meant to work together. Maybe trying to fit a square peg into a round hole is not a good idea. Even without the Next Gen running day-to-day affairs, the family business will survive. There are lots of examples out there. And yet, wouldn't it be nice if father and daughter could work together, if they could learn how to give each other enough space to continue to grow?

He wasn't unreasonable. He recognized her unique talents.

He told himself that he understood the Next Gen's peculiarities.

It was too bad that he and his daughter did not always see eye-to-eye. No doubt, she still had a lot to learn and he was too impatient.

He wanted her to succeed. He wanted her to get ready to take over when his time was up.

Succession is the elephant in the room. Nobody wants to talk about it, but it's there and it keeps coming closer. The Current Gen drops a word, lets out a sigh; the Next Gen pretends not to hear, quickly changes the subject. The whole idea of succession is based on untested assumptions: about mutual readiness, about mutual desire and about mutual agreement. Unknowable until tried out and then very hard to reverse, that's what makes it so scary. It seems like all or nothing, not the kind of bet a prudent businessperson likes to take. On-the-job training is supposed to improve the odds, the more varied and the more challenging, the better for the business.

She saw no way out.

He thought hard work was the answer to every problem.

'Talk to him,' said her mother; 'Talk to her,' said his wife.

'Tell each other how you feel,' said a consultant.

Talking about it is always supposed to be the right thing to do. What if parent and child, father and adult daughter, don't know how to talk to each other? They talk all the time, why shouldn't they be able to talk to each other about how they feel? That's what the consultant is for, after all. Father never liked talking about his emotions; daughter knows that talking about feelings – hers and his – makes father uncomfortable.

This time, she would say no.

This time, he would find an alternative.

It's never a bad idea to get some distance, even if distance is hard to come by in the family business. Going to the same restaurants, being invited to the same parties, knowing the same people, the generations are likely to bump into each other every so often; coming together at family gatherings, Sunday lunches at mother's or Saturday cocktails with uncles and aunts, they are also likely to talk shop, even if they took a solemn vow not to do so. After all, the family is the business and the business is the family. Still, if you're of the Next Gen there's a lot to be said for doing your own thing: prove to yourself that you can do it on your own and get your confidence back. You don't need the family business; it needs you. Of course, distance makes the heart grow fonder and all. Father hears about how daughter is doing and wishes she would reconsider. Daughter hears about how father is doing and wonders if she made the right decision. So, is this just a typical father/daughter story? Will she come back to the family fold? Will he ever change? If there is going to be a next time, what will it look like?

Next time would be different.

Daughter and father, both, looked forward to next time.

The conceptual approach

In this chapter, we want to go beyond communication and delve into the sense of obligation that permeates parent/child relationships. The sense of obligation between parents and children is reciprocal but not symmetric. Parents owe their children protection and planning for the future; children, in turn, owe their parents loyalty and care in old age. In the family business context, this reciprocal sense of obligation means that many Current Gens expect Next Gens to join them in the family business, while, on the other hand, many Next Gens feel they 'have to' take on a role in the family business. Crucially, these expectations are typically left unstated, taken for granted as family norms. Thus, the sense of obligation may be strongly felt by the Next Gen, even if the Current Gen does not make explicit demands on them. The Next Gen's perceived obligation to serve the family business adds a subtle but hard to penetrate layer of hierarchy to the relationship between generations and impedes the development of trust maturity. If both generations *must* work together as opposed to *wanting* to work together, there is less incentive for building trust in each other's judgement.

Understanding family obligations

A sense of obligation towards the family derives from the generalized importance of loyalty, a concept that psychologists have studied extensively. For researchers in psychology, loyalty to a group means 'internalizing the spirit of the group's expectations'.[1] Loyalty implies reliable, positive attitudes towards the group. Crucially, it constitutes an internalized norm, a standard that is deeply held and not questioned. Loyalty is an essential building block of any set of durable relationships, of course, but particularly of family relationships. Loyalty to the family is well known to be particularly strong in Asian cultures.[2] However, there is ample psychological and sociological evidence to show that the norm of loyalty also plays an important role in Western cultures, especially where the multigenerational family is concerned.[3] Although the specific religious references and social frameworks differ across cultures, as do the political institutions, there is a shared emphasis on the importance of the family and the responsibility of family members to serve the family. Thus, both the Bible and the Koran, to say nothing of Confucius, make family loyalty a cornerstone of faith, a command that finds echoes in how very diverse societies sanction disloyalty to the family and how different legal structures, in turn, are set up to support the institution of the family. This is not to say that cultural differences are negligible or that loyalty to the family is felt and lived in the same way in different cultures. We also want to acknowledge that the existence of families that go across cultural boundaries (i.e. mixed marriages) and patchwork families makes it much more difficult to offer a single valid definition of what loyalty means in any particular case. Nonetheless, the relevance of obligation and loyalty persists.

How do obligation and loyalty play out in the family business of today? On the one hand, the Current Gen gives the Next Gen a lot of leeway in their education and development, much more than *they* ever had in their youth; the modern mantra is 'Do your own thing, find your passion.' Commonly, this mantra finds expression in parental payment for travel, university schooling and post-university entry into the job market, with few guidelines on what to study and where to work. Travel and study, often far from home, expose the Next Gen to new perspectives and new ideas, exposure that can ultimately turn out to be positive for the family business, but that can also distance the Next Gen from the family business. On the other hand, the Current Gen typically wants to ensure that their heirs have the training and experience to take over when the time comes. This desire grows as time advances and both generations get older; even if it is never stated explicitly or talked about as a quid pro quo, the burden of succession is on the Next Gen. Paradoxically, freedom can be given with ostensibly no strings attached, because loyalty to the family and to the family business seems to go without saying. This kind of inconsistency, if that is what it can be called, is inherently unstable, inviting misunderstanding and disappointment on both sides.

For their part, the Next Gen appreciate the freedom they have been given, but they also expect the freedom to study what they want and to live where they wish. In today's open society, where ideas and people travel so freely, the traditional methods of keeping the Next Gen at home and training them in the factory or in a customer's shop are no longer apposite or workable. In other words, today's freedom is seen as a right, not as a gift. At the same time, and for the reasons set out above in the discussion of family and loyalty, the Next Gen feel a strong sense of obligation. The difficulty for many Next Gens – even those who are not interested in or favourably predisposed towards the family business – is that working in the family business full time is often seen as the most viable way to satisfy both their parents' expectations and their own sense of doing right by the family.[4] This is not the case in every family business, but it is in many. As mentioned above, the Current Gen sees the Next Gen as their successors, the ones who will eventually take over, and being a successor requires working in the business; the Next Gen, in turn, internalizes the duty of succession and knows that this duty necessarily implies working in the business.

Family obligation and personal development

As mentioned in the introduction, we do not believe that all Next Gens or even the majority of Next Gens ought to work in the family business. In this context, the sense of obligation between parents and children can be a real impediment to personal development, for both parents and children and, ultimately, also for the family business. A feeling of obligation is not a good starting point for developing peer-based collaboration. Much better for the business and the family if those Next Gens who do not see a future for themselves in the family business stay out of it entirely. One reason why Next Gens who do not really want to work in the family business still wind up doing so has to do with the higher degree of respect often accorded to family members in the business, respect from the Current Gen. A second reason for the Next Gen to put personal inclinations aside and work in the family business is to protect their rights as shareholders. Both motivations – to gain respect and to protect their rights – can be traced back to the two generations' understanding of how to show loyalty and how to fulfil obligation. *Because* it is expected that the Next Gen join the family business, *not* joining the family business can go together with reduced respect and abridged rights. While the question of Next Gen rights (i.e. as shareholders) can and should be solved by legal agreement, the matter of respect goes to the heart of the dilemma created by giving family members the freedom to decide their own course. Simple to say, but difficult to stick to, all family members deserve the same amount of respect, no matter what their career choice.

To be fair, the Next Gen's motivation for joining or re-joining the family business is rarely 100 per cent attributable to their sense of obligation. Generally, other reasons, such as greater entrepreneurial freedom and better career advancement possibilities, also play important roles in their decision. Unlike business reasons that have to withstand a reality test, however, loyalty is unquestioning. This leads many members of the Next Gen to stay in the family business much longer than they otherwise would, even if a career in the business is not satisfying, not successful, or neither. The reverse side of the loyalty coin is that the Current Gen may hold on to the vision of having the Next Gen in the business long after their time together has proven a poor fit. As difficult as it is, the Current and the Next Gens owe it to each other and to the business to be very honest in their assessment of suitability, loyalty to the family and dreams for a fairytale succession aside. In principle, being a member of the ownership family in a family business comes with a great many freedoms, in terms of financial capacity and the sheer variety of choices available. It is up to the individual and the family to ensure that these freedoms can be used, while still remaining true to the sense of obligation that is part and parcel of family life.[5]

Addressing the obligation/loyalty trap

The obligation/loyalty trap cannot be wished away; it is hardwired into family life and family business.[6] Talking about it may clarify feelings, but deeply held beliefs are hard to shift. Working with it means not taking anything for granted, not the Current Gen's commitment to helping the Next Gen and not the Next Gen's sense of obligation to supporting the Current Gen. How to go from obligation to aspiration? It starts with building a shared sense of purpose and belief in the desirability of maintaining the family business. If the business is to stay in the family, some if not all family members have to agree to take on key roles and make distinct contributions. In the best scenario, the Current Gen shows the Next Gen why being a part of the family business is desirable, and the Next Gen shows the Current Gen why they deserve to be invested in.

In fact, many family businesses are already doing a lot in this direction: family gatherings that explain what the business is about and make even children and young adults feel a part of something bigger; family activities (i.e. philanthropy, sports or music) that go beyond the business to build cohesion and excitement; and formal business presentations that bring everybody with a right to know up to date with not only the latest results but also the most promising projects. These various programmes fulfil important functions: information, connectedness and motivation. In order to prevent event overload and fatigue, it is essential to involve family members, and especially young members, in the planning: not obligation, but aspiration, with family members seeing themselves as co-producers, not as consumers. Equally important is a focus on high standards and accountability: every programme and every event can aim to improve on the last, with family members of the Current and the Next Gens holding each other accountable for the quality of what is produced.

Articulating multiple paths to contributing to the family business

In line with the focus on quality in programmes building aspirations, but more fundamental in terms of formal structure, both the Current Gen and the Next Gen are called upon to articulate multiple paths to contributing in meaningful ways to the family and the business, beyond full-time employment in the family business: the ownership committee, the board of directors of the business, the family council and the family charity (often in the legal form of a foundation), to name just a few of the many options available. It is not a matter of creating places to park family members of the Next Gen who do not want to or are not able to work full time in the family business. It is about creating options that are valued (read 'respected') by the family, where family members who do not work in the business can still make their contribution.

The Next Gen is called upon to fill these decision-making bodies for the family with life, to make the most of the various roles open to them by virtue of their membership of the family. Again, and in the best of cases, the emphasis is on building a process that involves people, not on filling positions in a chart. Where such decision-making bodies already exist, the task is often to make the work more desirable and more influential. Often, a family council or a family foundation need a reboot, with the Next Gen in a perfect position to get things going again. Where they do not already exist, the Next Gen can take a leading role in working out the briefs and job descriptions, based on best practice in other families (see also Chapter 8). There is a lot of good work being done on these questions – by other families, with or without the help of consultants – that any family with the interest to do so can benefit from.

Efforts to motivate *voluntary* cooperation do not end once the Next Gen finds its place in the family business. Just as the sense of obligation remains, so does the work of going beyond obligation and inspiring aspiration go on, involving both generations in a reciprocal process of give and take. Every step of the way, family members challenge each other to get better and to do more. Over years of working together in various capacities, assumptions about obligation and loyalty are replaced by self-confident assertions of preferences about what kind of work to do and who to work with. The family business may at times appear to be a golden cage, but it does not have to be a psychological closed circle where the inmates are condemned to repeat the same behaviours over and over again. The key is to learn to see the family business as the fulcrum of a growth process, for both the Next Gen and the Current Gen.

KEY TAKEAWAYS

1. In many family businesses, both of the generations face an obligation/loyalty trap.
2. The key to overcoming the obligation/loyalty trap is voluntary cooperation.
3. Paths for contributing to the family and the family business are multiple.

Learning journey: Pit stop 2

Please refer to Chapter 12 for a full explanation of the educational approach supporting the learning journey.

SELF-LEARNING

Self-assessment

Assess where you and the other generation are and should be on the continuum between obligation and aspiration.

Self-reflection

Current Gen: Think through the following statements. How true are they of your own situation?

Members of the Next Gen know what I expect of them.

I don't put pressure on the Next Gen. They are free to choose.

Working in the business is only one of many ways to contribute to the family.

Next Gen: Think through the following statements. How true are they of your own situation?

The Current Gen is almost impossible to satisfy.

I feel a lot of pressure to live up to expectations. I'm not free.

Working in the business is the only way to contribute to the family.

Development plan for Current Gen/Next Gen

Draw up a development plan in which you define the following milestones:

Short term: What will I do by next week to close the obligation/aspiration gap? What will I consider a success by then?

Medium term: What will I do by next month to close the obligation/aspiration gap? What will I consider a success by then?

Long term: What will I do by next year to close the obligation/aspiration gap? What will I consider a success by then?

Action review

Mark the dates in your calendar when you check how well you have achieved the short-, medium- and long-term goals you set. Evaluate what you have achieved and look back at what went well and what went poorly.

MODERATED WORKSHOP LEARNING

Group discussion

Use the material presented in Chapter 2 as a launch pad for thinking about and critically discussing how the family approaches loyalty and obligation.

For the Current Gen, first prepare yourself, then discuss with the Next Gen:

What do you expect the Next Gen to contribute to the family business (time, skills, roles)?

For the Next Gen, first prepare yourself, then discuss with the Current Gen:

How do you want to contribute to the family business? What do the Current Gen expect from you (time, skills, roles)?

Case discussion

Read fictional case 2 and discuss the following questions:

Put yourself in the position of the daughter: what are her issues with father and family? What should she do?

Put yourself in the position of the father: what are his expectations? What can he do to reset the relationship?

As a consultant to the family, (how) would you advise daughter and father to voice their unspoken feelings?

Case simulation

Replay the conversation between the daughter and her father in your own words.

For the Next Gen, assume the role of the father.

For the Current Gen, assume the role of the daughter.

Starting positions: daughter confronts father about assuming readiness/meddling; father demands commitment to the family business.

Those who are not involved in the simulation observe and comment.

Development plan for Current Gen/Next Gen

Draw up a development plan in which you define the following milestones:

Short term: What will I do by next week to close the obligation/aspiration gap? What will I consider a success by then?

Medium term: What will I do by next month to close the obligation/aspiration gap? What will I consider a success by then?

Long term: What will I do by next year to close the obligation/aspiration gap? What will I consider a success by then?

Co-coaching

Choose a partner from a different generation and share your development plan with him or her. Arrange two follow-up meetings after two months and after six months to see how well you have implemented your plan.

CLASSROOM LEARNING

Group discussion

Use the material presented in Chapter 2 as a launch pad for thinking about and critically discussing how families approach loyalty and obligation.

What conditions help the Next Gen to regard their future role as an aspiration rather than an obligation?

What may get in the way of the Next Gen regarding their future role as an aspiration rather than an obligation?

Case discussion

Read fictional case 2 and discuss the following questions:

> *Put yourself in the position of the daughter: what are her issues with father and family? What should she do?*
>
> *Put yourself in the position of the father: what are his expectations? What can he do to reset the relationship?*
>
> *As a consultant to the family, (how) would you advise daughter and father to voice their unspoken feelings?*

Case simulation

Replay the conversation between the daughter and her father in your own words.

Starting positions: daughter confronts father about assuming readiness/meddling; father demands commitment to the family business.

Those who are not involved in the simulation observe and comment.

Oxford-style debate

Form two teams and prepare to debate the following thesis, with one team in favour and the other team against:

> Aligning the Next Gens' aspirations with the needs of the family business will become increasingly challenging, as young people have more and more career options to choose from.

Conduct a debate to collect all possible and valid arguments for and against the proposal.

Case report

Choose a family business that you know or are familiar with and analyse how the Next Gen attempts to align their personal aspirations with the needs of the family business. Make concrete suggestions on how this alignment can be facilitated.

From conflictual rivalry to negotiated accord 03

Apply fair process

CASE STUDY

Fictional case 3

Classic father/son dynamics. Father started the business, built it up from scratch, directs the production process from A to Z, works with a veteran team of confidantes, knows each and every one of the customers – it's his baby. First-born son grows up with the business, takes on various roles in the business, goes abroad to study and comes back, but wants to make his own mark. Younger sister and younger brother have already found their comfort zones in the family business, sister in accounts, brother in production, complementing father perfectly. Father is a local institution, has the ear of ministers and industry leaders. Emerging markets, frequent ups and frequent downs, riddled with relational complications, but full of exciting opportunities to start new ventures, in the home country, as well as in the greater region. Personal network and access to capital are essential. First-born son fights to get out from under the shadow of father, but father holds the keys to so many doors. Classic father/son dynamics with a twist.

'Stay away from my business! You'll ruin it.'

How many times have I heard him say that. No matter what I do, I can never win him over. Getting the best grades in school, beating out all the other kids in sports, being the responsible one when my siblings had their party years, it was all for him. And that was only the beginning. What I haven't tried since then. I don't know why I care so much.

'Don't you see that I'm only trying to help? The business needs to have professional structures… come on, accounts are still manual, IT runs on Excel, HR is your schoolfriend's daughter... we're too big for that. You can't keep holding the whole thing together with tape and glue.'

'You don't understand how things work; you're not an engineer.'

There it is again, the E-word. It's like a curse hanging over me. What do engineers have that I don't have? Rational, check; logical, check; methodical, check. Not every engineer is a great businessman, not every great businessman is an engineer. Just because I'm not an engineer, my opinions don't count?

'Engineering built this business, I appreciate that, I really do… but it won't take us to the next level; what we need now is organization and strategy, you know, things like cutting down on duplication, setting sales targets and planning for the future… that's what I'm good at, that's where I can help.'

'What business have you built? Big ideas, sure, but results? Show me results.'

He always expected a great deal from me, first-born and all. He set higher hurdles for me than for my siblings… or maybe I set myself higher hurdles. He took risks to start this business – all of his money, all of his time, putting his name on the line, but he always had a way out. I don't. If I really want to make it on my own, I have to take even bigger risks than he did – it's got to be all or nothing.

'I just want a fair chance, I'm not asking for more than that. Why can't you give me a fair chance?'

'You're a dreamer… dreaming is what you're good at.'

The truth is, the family business – the business he built – doesn't interest me all that much. Yes, it could do with process improvements and professionalization at all levels, but, no, it's not a matter of life-and-death. The business is good enough to just keep on rolling and my siblings are around to make sure of that. It'll take time, but they'll eventually convince him to make the necessary changes. I'm not a company man, I'm an entrepreneur, I was born to be an entrepreneur… started selling things in school, even before university, I was hatching fully fledged business plans; one thing after another since then, first in gas, then in water, not a day goes by when I don't think of something new, my mind is always on – full throttle.

'I've got a plan for a new investment that I wanted to talk to you about. Thanks to a friend of a friend, I have the chance to buy into a real estate project on the North Shore. It's an up-and-coming area – you must have heard about it. They want to build a high-end residential complex of one hundred units; it'll have a concierge service, a top-of-the-line spa, two restaurants, all the amenities. The price is right; it's an opportunity too good to be missed.'

'Another new business... what about the natural gas venture, what happened to that? Or the sweet water project? Every time, it costs a lot of money; every time, it's the next big thing. What do you know about real estate, or construction, for that matter?

'Hear me out. It's different this time.'

'The trouble with you is... you don't know how to start small and stick with it.'

He did it on a shoestring. He didn't have a choice and that's just the way it was in those days. Today, you need a lot of money and the best people to be able to move quickly. If you don't get in first and stake a serious claim, somebody else will. Speed is the name of the game and speed will cost you. He just doesn't understand how the new world works.

'Small doesn't cut it these days. You have to go big.'

'Go big with somebody else's money... not my money.'

When it's for his business, the business that he started, it's our money; when it's for my projects, it's his money. I wish I didn't have to beg like this every time. It's just so humiliating. It'll be my money one day, at least part of it, so why not let me have my share now? Why does he have to keep on treating me like a little kid? End of the day, he just doesn't trust me.

'I've been too easy on you... people warned me.'

'I'll prove you wrong. You're going to regret talking to me like this.'

My friends tell me to give up, to strike out on my own – in a different country, in a completely different field. Maybe I should. Go to New York, join up with some of my mates from business school, cook up a business plan and run with it. Funding? We'll work the venture capital circuit. It's tough as hell over there, but at least the Americans recognize entrepreneurs and know how to value breakthrough ideas. I should never have come back.

'You can't make it on your own; you need me.'

'I don't see why the rules are not the same for me, why you support my sister and my brother... but you won't support me.'

'Your sister, your brother... they don't come in here asking for help every other day.'

'Don't try to pit my siblings against me.'

'Feet on the ground, nose to the grindstone… they're like me; you're not.'

'How dare you?'

Every time it's the same thing, he really knows how to push my buttons. Everything they are and I'm not, at least in his eyes. Why can't he stop comparing, why does he have to make it a contest among the three of us? This time, I won't let him get to me. I'll be the mature one; I'll be the one in charge. I'm not going to allow anybody to play with me anymore, not even him. I've had enough of his games.

'This is turning into a shouting match. I've got to go.'

'Go, go, you'll be back.'

He's right. Five years since he died and I keep coming back.

The conceptual approach

The family business can be a hotbed of conflictual rivalry: parent/child, father/son, mother/daughter and, of course, sibling rivalry. Indeed, for some observers, the struggle over power is *the* defining characteristic of the family business.[1] Interpersonal rivalries exist everywhere, in politics, in academia, in business, too, of course, but what makes rivalries in family business particularly salient is the character of the inner circle: first, family members have all known each other for a long time and whatever tensions that exist may have had a chance to fester for years; second, because the circle decides over matters that have to do with the family business and the family, rivalries over rights and benefits concern everyone in the family; third, and perhaps most important in an intergenerational context, the biological certainty that one generation will eventually replace the other makes rivalries take on an existential feel. In other words, in family business, common rivalries between and among individuals are amplified: like an echo chamber, a family business can become a closed system in which conflictual rivalry drowns out everything else.

Understanding rivalry in the family business

Let us examine the different forms of family business rivalry in turn, starting with the rivalry between the Current Gen and the Next Gen, the best known and most common of all rivalries, not only in family business, but probably also more generally. Like in the time of the ancient Greeks, and as recounted in the tales of Zeus and Oedipus, the Next Gen can feel blocked by the Current Gen, and the Current Gen can feel threatened by the Next Gen.[2] As we pointed out in the introduction, Freud took Sophocles' classical *Oedipus* story as a point of reference for a neurosis, the son's jealousy of the father and the father's fear of the son, and it became one of the pillars of modern psychology. Even though Freud's overreliance on this lens has been heavily criticized and demystified, the fundamental psychological impact of the relationship cannot be denied. On the contrary, jealousy and fear appear in a variety of forms – the son's jealousy not only of the father's position vis-à-vis the mother, but also of the father's achievements; the father's fear not only of being outdone, but also the fear of death.

The Greeks may have made it a household name, but the father/son or parent/child rivalry is still very much with us in the family business of today, primed by the altered demographics of the elder and the changed perspectives of the younger to last longer and be felt more strongly than ever. In the family business, the rivalry between parent and child often takes the form of a contest over who is (to be) in control of the mutual asset, initially only a part of the business, but eventually the whole firm. Often, these struggles play out over strategic choices, such as where to invest or what areas to focus on, but the real conflict may be much deeper. Under these circumstances, a peer-based, side-by-side relationship is very difficult to achieve. As we will explain in Chapter 7, the Current Gen declaring 'Wait your turn' doesn't work very well when they are staying in power for longer than in the past and the Next Gen is signalling 'I'm ready now' earlier. Where talking about succession is taboo, as it is in many family businesses, and succession planning is not on the agenda, the natural rivalry may be even further accentuated. Reinforced by hierarchical structures in the business, the classical parent/child rivalry has the potential to be very destructive, if unchecked. Sophocles would find may fresh examples to write about if he were around today and took an interest in family businesses.

The mythical roots of sibling rivalry and its complement, branch rivalry, go back even further than those of the parent/child or father/son rivalry – in the Western tradition all the way back to the story of Cain and Abel in the Old Testament. As the story of Cain and Abel reveals, how the parents treat the children and whether they favoured one over another, and how the children treat each other and what they did together in childhood, both play an important role in furthering or indeed reducing sibling rivalry. In addition, at least in the popular imagination, birth order also contributes to personality differences among the siblings and sibling rivalry.[3] In other words, even with the best of intentions it is very hard to avoid struggles between siblings, and any study of how the family works has to include an examination of the relationships not just across but also within the generations.

How does all this psychological baggage affect the family business? First of all, sibling rivalry is broadly acknowledged to affect how the family business functions.[4] Not surprisingly, not a few high-profile past and present cases of family business dysfunction can be traced to sibling rivalries, for example the Gucci brothers in Italy or the Ambani brothers in India. Although they may be carried out in the business and purported to be about the future of the business, these intra-family rivalries are often only peripherally related to valid questions of strategy or operations. Instead, they usually amount to contests for power: attempts to maintain an old hierarchy among the siblings or to impose a new hierarchy. Like parent/child rivalry, sibling rivalry is inherent to families, and hence also to family businesses. The question is, what should be done about these rivalries so that they don't impair or, in the worst case, cripple the family business?

Although intra-family rivalries have a bad reputation and are often very painful, rivalry per se is not unhealthy. After all, business itself is built on rivalry, and competition is the basis of innovation. If carried out fairly, as an unbiased competition for the best ideas, then rivalry can be good for business: the best plan/project/person wins out. In the ideal case, rivalry pushes rival individuals to find more and better information to support their arguments. Particularly where decisions are not clear-cut and require a variety of inputs, the quality and diversity of information brought to bear are very important, and the presence of many voices makes it less likely that the family overlooks essential points. Rivalry expressed in a competition of ideas can also be a powerful antidote to groupthink, as active rivals are less likely than non-rivals to avoid conflict and submit to the herd instinct, provided that hierarchy doesn't stifle opposition.[5] If based on personality clashes or favouritism rather than objective differences of opinion, however, rivalry can harm business: not the best, but the best placed, wins out. Peer-based collaboration between the generations necessarily involves jousting over ideas and challenging each other about the assumptions and the data that underlie important decisions in the family business. The key is to be able to make use of rivalry and indeed competition in the family to positive ends.

The negative effects of rivalry based on personal conflicts

Many rivalries playing out in family businesses are distinctly personal. This means that personal reasons, not business reasons, are at the heart of the observed conflicts. Even personal rivalries, however, are often dressed up in business terms. Thus, a father or mother may vaunt his/her achievements and belittle the Next Gen's lack of a track record while dismissing new ideas, for example. More often than not, a private, subjective motivation runs beneath the conflict. This motivation may be conscious or unconscious, rooted in concrete events or multi-layered sentiments. In any case, conflictual rivalry based on personal feelings has many faces. Sometimes, it is right at the surface, ready to explode whenever there is an issue of contention. In other contexts, conflictual rivalry is subtler, expressing itself in behaviours like meddling, second-guessing or badmouthing, between the generations *and* within the generations. These kinds of behaviour sap energy from the family business. While personal conflicts and family quarrels are deeply human and can never be entirely eliminated or worked around, they are not a good basis for sustainable collaboration.

Winning a personal conflict is also a way to impose or maintain hierarchy. One side comes away as the loser and submits to the other. Even if the conflict is ostensibly about a business decision, i.e. an investment or a key hiring, personal animosities can make it feel like it's ultimately about putting someone in their place. Favouritism, when it comes up in situations of interpersonal rivalry, cements hierarchy. No matter what a disfavoured individual does, he/she will always lose out to the favoured family member or even the favoured non-family member. Ultimately, making decisions based on personal bias and the desire to maintain power can dangerously undermine the willingness of family members, especially members of the Next Gen, to commit their full energies to the family business. Truly peer-based collaboration only takes root and blossoms where rivalry and competition within the family are based on objective standards, fairly administered.

Fair process in the family business

What does fair process mean? In the context of the family business and intergenerational collaboration, fair process means '(1) communication and voice; (2) clarity of information, process and expectations; (3) consistency across people, over time, and with agreed values and norms; (4) changeability of decisions, process, goals and principles; and (5) commitment to fairness'.[6] Fair process means equal consideration for all and is not to be confused with equal outcomes for all; a process can be fair, even if one party loses and another party wins. In effect, both winners and losers benefit from fair process – a fair process builds and maintains belief in the system as a whole. In a fair process, underlying assumptions are surfaced and competing ideas are given equally careful consideration. The winning idea or proposition is not automatically the one offered by the most powerful or the most favoured player: in a fair competition, anyone can win. Fair competition is the essence of successful peer-based collaboration.

It is worth noting that the ability to have adult conversations (discussed in Chapter 1) and the capacity for understanding and addressing the sense of obligation between generations (described in Chapter 2) are essential prerequisites for implementing fair process in the family business. In fact, fair process is substantially based on open dialogue and clearly expressed expectations. Fair process works when the generations know how to communicate with each other on an even playing field and put objective business concerns over feelings of loyalty. In other words, getting to fair process is not a simple matter of applying a recipe and robotically following a few rote steps. Rather, the successful application of fair process is a sign that the family has come quite a distance in developing the building blocks of peer-based collaboration. It should go without saying that fair process is not the solution to all the complications that can plague family interaction; deep-seated psychological tensions in particular are very difficult to overcome without focused attention and, sometimes, external help. A consistent lack of fair process, on the other hand, will almost certainly exacerbate existing conflicts in the family and prevent effective collaboration.

Good and bad competition inside the family

What's the difference between good competition and bad competition inside the family? Is it merely a question of what is good for the business? Competition among individuals is endemic to business organization: competition over resources, competition over roles and competition over power. In family businesses, competition over power can be particularly pronounced, as it goes beyond the organizational and affects the personal: those who are in power often have sway over the family assets and hence also, at least to some degree, over the individual freedom of all family members.[7] In many family businesses, the individual(s) at the top of the family pyramid set the rules for the others; this can lead to significant restrictions on how family members live their lives.[8] In other words, and when compared with other forms of business ownership, the stakes in the power game played in the family business are especially high. Even if parent/child rivalry and sibling rivalry were not baked in to the family business as they are, it would still be a hotbed of competing interests and competing aspirations.

Accordingly, competition inside the family is rarely only about what is good for the business, and it plays out in many different arenas. Decision-making about business matters, i.e. investments, projects and jobs, is only one of the arenas to consider when working to defuse conflict in the family business. A non-comprehensive list of subjects with conflict potential for the business family would include: personal wealth vs family wealth; employment policy for family members; resentment among branches; personal animosity.[9] If the family business has existed for many years, these subjects of conflict may have gone unresolved for a long time and be deeply engrained in the fabric of family interactions. In the ideal case, they are treated separately, outside of discussions focused on the business. Given their own space, questions about wealth, employment and branch relations will also benefit from the application of fair process. Even with the best intentions and the most careful attention to insulating decision processes, however, it is almost impossible to avoid getting these non-business questions mixed up with business questions. Again, conflict is better acknowledged and addressed than swept under the table.

Conflict and rivalry do not disappear with use of fair process and the effort to reach negotiated accord, but they are defused and channelled. As we will discuss in Chapter 8, the absence or the inadequacy of corporate governance is often to blame if power struggles in the family business get out of hand. Establishing fair process as a culture of interaction is an important part of the picture, but fair process cannot substitute for a well-built and broadly accepted corporate governance structure. In a functioning corporate governance structure, there are clear rules of engagement, guidelines for who gets involved when, and parameters for making important decisions that concern all shareholders, including decisions related to succession (cf. Chapter 9). In some cases, learning how to work with fair process can be a stepping-stone to installing corporate governance; more generally, fair process is an essential ingredient in making corporate governance work and keeping it alive through the ups and downs of the business and the family.

KEY TAKEAWAYS

1. Conflictual rivalry between and within generations is characteristic of family business.
2. Rivalry over issues reinvigorates the business; rivalry over people saps the business.
3. Fair process helps resolve conflictual rivalry and motivates focused collaboration.

Learning journey: Pit stop 3

Please refer to Chapter 12 for a full explanation of the educational approach supporting the learning journey.

SELF-LEARNING

Self-assessment

Assess where you and the other generation are and should be on the continuum between conflictual rivalry and negotiated accord.

Self-reflection

Current Gen: Think through the following statements. How true are they of your own situation?

Rivalries between Current Gen and Next Gen don't play a significant role for us.

There is an established process for addressing family disagreements.

Every member of the family is treated fairly and equally.

Next Gen: Think through the following statements. How true are they of your own situation?

Rivalries between Current Gen and Next Gen do play a significant role for us.

There is no established process for addressing family disagreements.

Some members of the family are treated better/worse than others.

Development plan for Current Gen/Next Gen

Draw up a development plan in which you define the following milestones:

Short term: What will I do by next week to close the conflict/negotiation gap? What will I consider a success by then?

Medium term: What will I do by next month to close the conflict/negotiation gap? What will I consider a success by then?

Long term: What will I do by next year to close the conflict/negotiation gap? What will I consider a success by then?

Action review

Mark the dates in your calendar when you check how well you have achieved the short-, medium- and long-term goals you set. Evaluate what you have achieved and look back at what went well and what went poorly.

MODERATED WORKSHOP LEARNING

Group discussion

Use the material presented in Chapter 3 as a launch pad for thinking about and critically discussing how the family approaches rivalry and conflict.

For the Current Gen, first prepare yourself, then discuss with the Next Gen:

What anecdotes best describe the rivalries and struggles for power in your family, between the generations and within the generations?

For the Next Gen, first prepare yourself, then discuss with the Current Gen:

What anecdotes best describe the rivalries and struggles for power in your family, between the generations and within the generations?

Case discussion

Read fictional case 3 and discuss the following questions:

Put yourself in the position of the father: what would it take for the son to convince the father of his merit?

Put yourself in the position of the son: how can the son work his way out of his dependence on the father?

As a consultant to the family, (how) would you advise father and son to resolve their differences and build trust?

Case simulation

Replay the conversation between the son and his father in your own words.

For the Next Gen, assume the role of the father.

For the Current Gen, assume the role of the son.

Starting positions: son lists his personal challenges; father lists his preconceptions; both try to find common ground.

Those who are not involved in the simulation observe and comment.

Development plan for Current Gen/Next Gen

Draw up a development plan in which you define the following milestones:

Short term: What will I do by next week to close the conflict/negotiation gap? What will I consider a success by then?

Medium term: What will I do by next month to close the conflict/negotiation gap? What will I consider a success by then?

Long term: What will I do by next year to close the conflict/negotiation gap? What will I consider a success by then?

Co-coaching

Choose a partner from a different generation and share your development plan with him or her. Arrange two follow-up meetings after two months and after six months to see how well you have implemented your plan.

CLASSROOM LEARNING

Group discussion

Use the material presented in Chapter 3 as a launch pad for thinking about and critically discussing how families approach rivalry and conflict.

What are the root causes of conflictual rivalry in family business?

What are the key pitfalls to avoid, so as to prevent or diminish conflictual rivalry in family business?

Case discussion

Read fictional case 3 and discuss the following questions:

Put yourself in the position of the father: what would it take for the son to convince the father of his merit?

Put yourself in the position of the son: how can the son work his way out of his dependence on the father?

As a consultant to the family, (how) would you advise father and son to resolve their differences and build trust?

Case simulation

Replay the conversation between the son and his father in your own words.

Starting positions: son lists his personal challenges; father lists his preconceptions; both try to find common ground.

Those who are not involved in the simulation observe and comment.

Oxford-style debate

Form two teams and prepare to debate the following thesis, with one team in favour and the other team against:

A certain degree of rivalry between the Current and Next Gen is not only unavoidable but also leads to better outcomes, given its competitive character.

Conduct a debate to collect all possible and valid arguments for and against the proposal.

Case report

Choose a family business that you know or are familiar with and analyse how conflictual rivalry unfolds. Make concrete suggestions on how to achieve negotiated accords

PART TWO
Capability appreciation
Strategic thinking

As regards your business plans for the future, my son, I rejoice in the lively interest they indicate, without being able entirely to agree with them. You start with the idea that the market for our native products – for instance, grain, rapeseed, hides and skins, wool, oil, oilcake, bones, etc. – is our chief concern; and you think it would be of advantage for you to turn yourself to the commission branch of the business. I once occupied myself with these ideas, at a time when the competition was small (it has since distinctly increased), and I made some experiments in them. My journey to England had for its chief purpose to look out connections there for my undertakings. To this end I went as far as Scotland and made many valuable acquaintances; but I soon recognized the precarious nature of an export trade hither and decided to discourage further expansion in that direction. Thus I kept in mind the warning of our forefather, the founder of the firm, which he bequeathed to us, his descendants: 'My son, attend with zeal to thy business by day, but do none that hinders thee from thy sleep at night.'

THOMAS MANN, *BUDDENBROOKS: THE DECLINE OF A FAMILY* (1901)

This excerpt from Thomas Mann's *Buddenbrooks*, the only book about business ever to be recognized in the citation for the Nobel Prize in Literature, explicitly mentions two of the three themes we will be focusing on in Part Two, legacy vs change and practice vs theory, and hints at the third, internal vs external. Actually, these themes run throughout *Buddenbrooks*. The family's failure to evolve with the times and make the most of each generation's unique capabilities counts for a lot in the ultimate decline of the Buddenbrooks' family business. Of course, it is in the nature of a novel to dramatize differences between the generations and emphasize conflict over harmony. Nonetheless, the fact that the book continues to be relevant over 120 years after its publication, even constituting required reading for some business families, means that Thomas Mann was able to touch upon a set of universal truths. Inasmuch as they concern the capacity of the Current Gen and the Next Gen to appreciate each other's unique capabilities and the strategic thinking required for a family business to stay competitive in a rapidly changing environment, we want to explore these in greater depth. What are the strategically salient capabilities that the different generations bring to the table?

By virtue of long years spent in the business, the Current Gen has more practical experience and a deeper knowledge of operations; the Next Gen, on the other hand, is likely to have more advanced academic training and often also broader international exposure. These differences can serve the family business, if the older and younger appreciate each other's knowledge bases and skills for what they are – not competing, but complementary. Building *capability appreciation* is the focus of Part Two. Like trust maturity, capability appreciation occurs at multiple levels. In the first place comes the classic juxtaposition of old and new, with the Current Gen more apt to hold on to legacy businesses and legacy methods, and the Next Gen more enthusiastic about embracing strategies for change (Chapter 4). The second juxtaposition facing the generations in family business pits practice versus theory, what the Current Gen knows from having done it versus what the Next Gen knows from having learned about it, in school or in professional settings outside the family business and, more often than not, outside the home country (Chapter 5). The third level of capability appreciation has to do with the weight accorded to practices from inside and outside the family business (Chapter 6).

Learning approach: Side by side as strategic thinking

Adopting the side-by-side mindset to generational transition in the family business does not stop with the social psychology of developing trust maturity. Indeed, trust maturity provides the basis or starting point for taking advantage of contributions from both the Current Gen and the Next Gen to enhance the quality of strategic thinking in the family business. Strategic thinking in a family business differs from strategic thinking in a listed company because of the involvement of the owners. Whereas in a listed company shareholders are widely dispersed and do not get directly involved in strategy except under unusual circumstances (i.e. shareholder activism), shareholders in a family business are few and typically have a significant say in strategy, either as executives or as members of the board of directors. Along with a say in strategy comes a sense of responsibility for the business and this sense of responsibility often extends to the Next Gen, even before they formally assume shared ownership. Moreover, because the family business usually represents the vast majority of their wealth, shareholders in a family business, unlike shareholders in a listed company, express a preference for diversification *within* the business, as opposed to *across* investments. Taken together, these differences between the family business and the listed company imply that strategic thinking in the family business involves active participation in maintaining the long-term quality of the asset over many years by an evolving group of closely related individuals. In other words, strategy is still strategy – the choice of markets and the allocation of resources in a given competitive context – but with the need to factor in the owners' particular sense of responsibility for the future and an adjusted set of objectives.

- **Point of departure**

  → *Strategy is about continuously creating new sources of competitive advantage*. Strategy is about the choice of markets and the allocation of resources in a given competitive context. While the tenets of this definition have remained in place essentially unchanged since the early days of the systematic study of strategic management in the 1970s, the pace at which strategy needs to be reviewed and revised has accelerated markedly. Where strategists of old could count on competitive advantage once achieved to last for a number of years, the speed of change in the business world of today means that any competitive advantage is fleeting.[1] Worse, whole industries have been subject to disruption and new threats are continuously emerging, dangerous even for the most strongly positioned businesses.[2] For the family business this means that strategy and, by extension, strategic thinking require a focus on creating new sources of competitive advantage. Instead of holding on to advantages from the past and planning on the basis of the supposedly stable present, today's strategy creates the future.

- **Important assumptions**

  → *Openness to change is better, in the long run, for sustaining the (family) business.* If today's strategy is about creating the future, then it is essential that the family business be open to change. In any business, creating the future necessarily builds on the past, combining old and new, existing and novel. This is where the side by side of the generations comes into play. Rather than being seen as a difficulty to be overcome, the difference in capabilities that separates the Current Gen and the Next Gen can be seen as an advantage or an opportunity to improve the quality of strategic thinking in the family business. In a sense, generational transition opens the doors to change, but if any meaningful change has to await formal leadership succession, it may be too late for the family business. Strategizing side by side, the Current Gen and the Next Gen have the chance to prepare the family business for continuous change and adaptation, in line with or even a step ahead of the evolution of the competitive context.

- **Normative implications**

  → *Build a strategy process to optimize the diverse capabilities of multiple generations.* At every level of leadership, ownership, board of directors and executive, the strategy process can be structured so as to take a variety of different viewpoints into consideration and to optimize the diverse capabilities of multiple generations. To do so effectively, it is first necessary to emphasize the importance of the strategy process; in many family businesses, the strategy process suffers from benign neglect, as decision-makers focus on getting the job done and the board of directors primarily serves the purposes of formal administration. Where the strategy process is recognized as critical, sufficient time is put aside for the discussion of strategic topics and the standards for strategic thinking are high. To ensure that the strategically salient capabilities of both the Current and the Next Gen can be brought to bear, every effort is made to place qualified representatives of the Next Gen on the relevant decision-making bodies as full members or at least observers, define their roles as valuable voices of change and set up strategic deliberations in such a way that the tough questions get ample space to be aired and debated.

From legacy vs change to legacy *and* change

04

Reassess goals

CASE STUDY

Fictional case 4

Imagine a village in pastoral Somerset in the UK: surrounded by a lot of green, of course, with rocky hills and continuously shifting skies. At the edge of the village, not far from the ancient Arms with its red window casings and hand-built stone walls, you will find the factory and headquarters of Rose Cheese, an industrial style building from the early 20th century. Too big for the village, really, Rose is a testament to the accomplishment and the perseverance of one local family, six generations of dedicated workers who have made the name of the village synonymous with cheese. Time to go into the factory and meet the family, starting with Uncle Jim and Uncle John, the octogenarian fourth generation leaders of Rose Cheese.

Still standing tall and straight, the uncles had manned their posts at the creamery every working day and on many weekends for the last sixty years. From a wrought-iron platform set above the cheese vats, they could observe every step in the production process. The elder of the two, Uncle Jim, took his place behind a well-polished mahogany captain's desk, the very desk that his great grandfather Angus, the founder of Rose Cheese, had purchased on the occasion of the birth of his first son. So that the two of them could have different views of what was going on below, Uncle John sat with his back to his brother, at a metal desk covered with files and papers. Uncle Jim was the engineer, the expert when it came to any question about production; Uncle John was the accountant, the man in charge of the numbers.

Uncle Jim missed the good old days, when workers and customers were less demanding, but still loved coming to the factory every morning and sitting down at old Angus's desk. Some thirty years ago, he had overseen the first modernization of the factory and he still marvelled at the quality of the equipment they had decided to install. Nobody in Somerset made better cheese and Uncle Jim wanted to make sure that it stayed that way for a long time to come. He hoped that his own grandson would one day be making wise decisions for Rose Cheese from behind the same glorious desk. Uncle John was all about habits and regularity: without fail, he entered the building at 8 am and left at 6 pm; nothing could keep him from his 9 am tour of operations or his 5 pm tipple; the rest of the day, he burrowed his face in the daily paper or pretended to study the company books. In his time, Uncle John had been a whiz at finance, watching every penny and securing funding to keep operations going during the business's most difficult years. Never promise what you can't deliver, always be prudent; that was his credo.

Just as the uncles had learned from their fathers, their children and adult grandchildren (the fifth and sixth generation of Roses) were now attending to the day-to-day business: purchasing cow's milk from local farmers, managing transport schedules, supervising the curdling, watching over the moulding and the bathing, inspecting maturation and, finally, administering regional distribution to specialty shops and grocers. Every step of the way, a Rose was involved. Of course, not every Rose had stayed in the village and devoted his or her life to cheese, but those who had stayed or had ventured out for education and experience and come back were good ones, with the energy and the commitment to take the business forward. The young ones were on the right track, the uncles often said to each other. For as long as they were still able, they planned to steer the Rose family fortunes, but when the time came for them to go, the Next Gens would be ready.

The craft of cheese making had remained essentially unchanged for centuries. Larger farms, yes, new machines, yes, different customers, yes, new regulations, also, but, at its core, Rose Cheese was still Rose Cheese, as created in the 19th century by Angus Rose. The uncles saw themselves as links in a long chain that went back to the founder and stretched forward into the distant future. They did not ignore changes in the industry – after all, it was under their leadership that the family had made unprecedented investments in manufacturing – they simply were not ready to throw everything overboard for new ideas about how to do business and vague promises of growth. Uncle Jim and Uncle John firmly believed that there would always be a market for good quality, basic varieties of English cheese and that Rose Cheese must continue to function as it always had. That's why they ignored the aches and pains of age and kept coming to their office overlooking the factory floor.

Rose Cheese stood still, but the cheese business moved on. Specialization, internationalization and digitization – every ten years or so, there had been a major shift in the business and the changes had a cumulative effect. End customers wanted something distinctive if they were going to pay more than the minimum price set by foreign competition; nationwide retailers also wanted distinctive products, but weren't willing to support local brands and demanded that producers pay for up-to-date logistics. It was becoming harder and harder for mid-sized, undifferentiated producers like Rose to survive. Not that bankers, lawyers and other friends of the family hadn't said their piece. They didn't like the fact that Rose Cheese had not experienced meaningful growth since the early 2000s and warned that the traditional business model was not sustainable. Not that the fifth generation of Roses hadn't tried to do things differently, and those few members of the sixth generation to stick with the family business hadn't rebelled. The fifth generation had focused on improved marketing, telling the Rose Cheese story and expanding the product range to include new varieties; the sixth generation, finally, proposed entering into partnership agreements with other local food companies in order to support international expansion, but secretly they started to question whether the family should even remain in the business of making cheese.

Discussions about where to go with the family business happened spontaneously and tended to be short and curt. As long as they were in charge, and the uncles spoke with one voice on this point, Rose Cheese would not go down any of these 'false new paths': too risky, too expensive, or too outlandish to even consider. Already in their late fifties and early sixties, the fifth generation did not have the energy anymore to disagree with their fathers. They just kept going because that's what they knew how to do best. The sixth gens who had chosen to begin their career in cheese were of a different breed: better educated than their predecessors, more audacious and a lot less patient. They saw Rose Cheese as an opportunity and were not satisfied with their uncles' dismissive answers. As a result, conflict between the sixth and the fourth generations was never far below the surface and could erupt at the drop of a hat. Anything could serve as a trigger for one or the other generation to pick up arms: a botched batch of curd, a missed delivery, or a complaint from a customer. The uncles liked to tell themselves and each other that the young ones were just being feisty, but deep down they understood that this generation was much harder to tame than their parents had been.

Two of the cousins eventually departed Somerset for a Masters course in London and did not return. Another young cheese maker, after failing to convince the uncles to provide him with a stipend for exploring new business opportunities, contacted a luxury hotel chain in Asia and left home to become Master of the Cheese Cellar at a five-star Singaporean hotel. The two sixth gens who decided to stay on, perhaps the least adventurous of the bunch, bided their time. The uncles would not live forever, they reasoned; one day, Rose Cheese would be theirs to work with. As disillusioned as they were, their fathers and mothers of the fifth generation would not stand in their way. It wasn't yet too late to make much needed changes to the business model, or, alternatively, to sell out for a reasonable sum, but with every passing year, the window of opportunity became smaller – both for Rose Cheese and, personally, for the two 21st century Roses who remained with the business. Despite the frequent disagreements they had with them, they could not help but respect the old uncles' steadfastness. Nevertheless, neither of them wanted to maintain the status quo indefinitely; neither of them wanted to wind up one day looking out at the world from behind beatified Angus's mahogany desk.

The conceptual approach

It would be too easy to say that the Current Gen stands for the status quo and the Next Gen stands for change. For one thing, there are always exceptions. Receptiveness to change is as much a function of entrepreneurial attitude as of age, and older entrepreneurs can be much more open to doing new things than younger family members with a conservative bent (see Chapter 7 and Chapter 10 for examples). Moreover, talking about the status quo and talking about change is not the same thing as sticking to the status quo when push comes to shove or actually carrying out the change. Nonetheless, in many cases, the traditional divide between the older and the younger is also reflected in how the generations approach the business. A key notion underlying this dynamic is the family legacy as it pertains to how to do business.[1] Typically, but not always, the Current Gen will put particular emphasis on preserving the family legacy, with statements like 'We stick to our knitting' and 'This is the way we do things around here', pre-empting discussions with the Next Gen about the scope of the business and quickly cutting off consideration of new methods. Although usually presented in the form of rational arguments that on the surface make good business sense, these perspectives typically belie a strong emotional attachment to the foundational building blocks of the business, the first products (or the legacy business) and the original processes and values (or the legacy way). It is the classic juxtaposition of tried and tested versus untried and novel, reinforced in the case of the family business by the weight of the ancestors.[2]

Understanding the power of legacy

The family legacy can be both a source of strength and a source of weakness – a strength because it underlines and attempts to preserve what is unique about the family firm, a weakness because it can prevent change and hold the business back.[3] One way around this dilemma is to embed change and innovation as values in the legacy, a practice observed in numerous cases.[4] Another way is to articulate the legacy so that it does not get in the way of change, when change in the business is needed, making it more about values and principles than about concrete business choices. In any case, the first step in dealing with the effect of legacy on the family business is to make it explicit and recognize its weight. This is especially important in the context of fostering intergenerational collaboration, because the Current Gen and the Next Gen will not necessarily have the same understanding and appreciation of the family legacy. The objective is to keep what is meaningful about the legacy without blocking innovation and change.

Business – any business – requires innovation to stay competitive. On the whole, as numerous studies have shown, family businesses are not more or less innovative than their established non-family counterparts in the same industry.[5] Innovation is difficult for any business and poses special challenges for the firm that has enjoyed past success and established a playbook for how to succeed. Prominent examples of this phenomenon could fill many pages and most, if not all, of these are not family firms: Kodak, IBM, Siemens, etc. Thus, Microsoft, a publicly listed firm, spent many years doggedly clinging to its winning formula of selling individual licences for software, even when its customers and its competitors – old and new – were transitioning to software in the cloud and by subscription. Legacy in family businesses includes the formula for past success(es) but also represents something more: admiration of the individuals who made it all possible and reverence for stories handed down from generation to generation, but also fear of losing everything that has been accumulated over time. For better or for worse, therefore, where the legacy business and the legacy way are concerned, family businesses tend to build in extra barriers to innovation and change, explicit rules and implicit assumptions. These barriers ensure that the business does not stray too far from the founding principles and are often used as tests for new ventures or novel methods.

Over time and across generations, the legacy can take on an absolute quality in some families, like a rule or a creed, and breaking out of it appears fraught with existential risk. The apocryphal question of what the founder would have thought can become a kind of prison that keeps the family and the family business locked in the (sometimes) distant past. At a time when competitive disruption is coming at established businesses from all angles and decisive action is necessary to take the business to the next level of competitive preparedness, a legacy carved in stone is debilitating. Instead of being open to change, the family business controlled by legacy is closed to change; instead of actively questioning and challenging its basis for success, in the most extreme cases it sticks its head in the sand of the past.

The family business in a world of rapid disruption

Contrast this view of the world with today's reality of rapid disruption. Inspired by the success stories of Facebook/Meta, Google/Alphabet, Netflix, Uber and many others, many business people today, and particularly younger people, believe that it is possible to make a big impact in a short time. Despite the statistical improbability of repeating these companies' feats, accelerated change has become the new normal, the new way of thinking about how to do business. How to reconcile the family legacy with accelerated change? It's not as if the Current Gen of family business leaders does not see what is happening around them. Everybody knows about Meta and Alphabet and everybody recognizes that these disruptors and others like them have replaced GM and GE at the top of the corporate pyramid. What everybody does not share, and what frequently separates the Next Gen from the Current Gen, is a visceral feeling for and a profound appreciation of a different way of doing business. Steeped as they often are in the family legacy, many members of the Current Gen cannot even conceive of pulling together a few like-minded people, renting the proverbial garage, raising capital from outside investors and setting out to launch a business that will change the world. Ironically, this picture is a pretty accurate representation of how a good part of the Next Gen thinks about the process of creating a business with the potential to make a big impact. We are exaggerating the contrast in world views, of course, but the differences are essential.

Family legacy as such provides one part of the explanation for why the Current Gen and the Next Gen find it difficult to see eye-to-eye on the question of what it takes to successfully run a business. By virtue of their ability to provide patient capital, family businesses tend to be more prevalent in capital-intensive sectors such as large-scale manufacturing (e.g. automobiles) or processing (e.g. traditional pharmaceuticals) with payoffs that are far into the future. The importance of personal assurance in activities like private banking, on the other hand, gives family businesses an edge of sorts in some relationship-focused industries. In emerging markets, we see many family businesses combining the advantages of patient capital and personal assurance to straddle multiple industries. Many of the most prominent contemporary examples of the new driving out the old, however, come from industries that rely primarily on human capital and operate in anonymous markets. This circumstance exacerbates the divide in how the Current Gen and the Next Gen think about business. Factories and apps are as hard to compare as the proverbial apples and oranges: as a result, the Current Gen and the Next Gen often fail to admit the relevance of their respective success narratives. It's like they are speaking two different languages. The truth, as always, lies somewhere in between. If effective change in the family business is to take place, the fresh input of the Next Gen is as important as the experience of the Current Gen. Without healthy respect for the legacy of the family business, a great deal of what makes the family business special is lost; without healthy disrespect for the legacy of the family business, there is a risk of remaining stuck in the past and, ultimately, failing to adapt to a rapidly changing competitive context.

New technologies arise out of novel combinations of existing technologies

In this debate between the generations, it is essential to take a step back and point out that new technologies arise out of novel combinations of existing technologies. As the economist W Brian Arthur has demonstrated in his remarkable book on the evolution of technology, new technologies do not simply hatch or emerge out of the ether; rather, a successful new technology represents an entrepreneurial response to changing economic needs, drawing on existing technological possibilities in unprecedented ways. In example after example, 'computer algorithms and beer brewing, power stations and pencils, hand-held devices and DNA sequencing',[6] Arthur shows that no matter how complex or simple the underlying technologies, their development is additive, with one step building upon the other. In the context of the family business these findings imply that legacy versus change should be seen as a false juxtaposition, a juxtaposition, moreover, that is likely to prevent adaptation. Just as the family business, or any other business for that matter, started by recombining existing technologies in new ways, the family business also evolves by adapting what is in the present to what is needed in the future. In this adaptation, both the Current and the Next Gen have an equally valid role to play, not to turn the family business into the next Meta or Alphabet by starting over from scratch, but to build on what works without letting the past dominate the present and obstruct the future.

Working together to combine the best of the existing and the new is one of the intergenerational challenges that benefits most from going through the developmental process described in Part One. Having gone through this process, both the Current and the Next Gens will be better able to understand and address the questions of legacy and renewal as peers: the ability to have adult conversations (Chapter 1) will prevent their interactions from degenerating into accusations of elder stubbornness and juvenile whim and, hopefully, lead to a better understanding of the family legacy; the capacity to go beyond a deeply felt, but unarticulated, sense of obligation to each other (Chapter 2) will enable the generations to build joint aspirations rather than remain in the groove of the past; finally, overcoming the sense of threat that characterizes so many relationships in business families will allow a fair and cool-headed appraisal of the merits of the case to take place, on the basis of what is needed to take the business forward in a world of accelerated change (Chapter 3).

Integrating legacy and change

In practice, legacy and change may not be as far apart as they seem at first glance. Positions that appear extreme in the abstract often soften when subjected to an experimental role reversal between the Current and Next Gens. Thus, it can be a worthwhile exercise for the Next Gen to think about how to make something new or do something in a new way out of know-how that already exists in the business. Can existing products be easily modernized by changing secondary features? Can an existing process be optimized by applying new technology? Conversely, the Current Gen may find it useful to work out how new knowledge – technological and commercial – might be applied to improve extant business practices. In other words, don't leave topics like new business models or digitalization of the supply chain to the Next Gen, but take the time to examine them in depth, involving the Next Gen as idea givers and consultants, as appropriate. The key idea here is 'in depth': too often, resolving legacy versus change flounders on the superficiality of the arguments. Blaming legacy on the one side and denying change on the other side can be more comfortable than getting your hands dirty and doing the work. In any case, and this is what Arthur's work also shows, any meaningful change only comes from assiduous application.

We wish to stress that not every change to the established way of doing things has to start with or lead to a competitive revolution of the type represented by the success stories of Meta and Alphabet. Indeed, many businesses have been founded and continued to thrive on continuous incremental improvement. It depends on the health of the business in question and on the competitive context, particularly the rate of change and the degree of rivalry. Slow and steady can be better than fast and drastic. However, in situations when radical transformation is absolutely necessary to ready the business for fundamentally new challenges or indeed save the business by giving it a major overhaul, both the Current and the Next Gens may wish to start by taking a long look at themselves in the mirror to determine whether or not they collectively have the means and the will to pull off the required changes. Sometimes, the legacy/change dilemma masks deeper problems that require assistance from outside the family business to resolve. The point is that every business from time to time needs a truly fresh look. Deeply ensconced in the day to day of operations and weighted down by personal experience and family legacy, the Current Gen is often not in the best position to provide that fresh look. Contrary to what one might imagine, however, the Next Gen also isn't necessarily well placed to offer a meaningfully different perspective – its understanding of how things work on the ground is often just not deep enough. Again, it is the interplay of the generations that promises the most insightful analysis and the most realistic chance for effective implementation of any transformation initiative or change programme.

KEY TAKEAWAYS

1. Legacy and change do not have to be opposites, but can work as complements.
2. Innovation arises out of new combinations of existing practices and technologies.
3. Role reversal is an effective technique for overcoming the legacy/change juxtaposition.

Learning journey: Pit stop 4

Please refer to Chapter 12 for a full explanation of the educational approach supporting the learning journey.

SELF-LEARNING

Self-assessment

Assess where you and the other generation are and should be on the continuum between legacy vs change and legacy and *change.*

Self-reflection

Current Gen: Think through the following statements. How true are they of your own situation?

The Next Gen doesn't care enough about preserving the legacy of the family.

Our legacy is a source of strength, not a hindrance to necessary change.

Change and innovation are part of our DNA as a business.

Next Gen: Think through the following statements. How true are they of your own situation?

The Current Gen is overly concerned about preserving the legacy of the family.

Our legacy is a source of weakness, a hindrance to necessary change.

Change and innovation are not part of our DNA as a business.

Development plan for Current Gen/Next Gen

Draw up a development plan in which you define the following milestones:

Short term: What will I do by next week to close the legacy/change gap? What will I consider a success by then?

Medium term: What will I do by next month to close the legacy/change gap? What will I consider a success by then?

Long term: What will I do by next year to close the legacy/change gap? What will I consider a success by then?

Action review

Mark the dates in your calendar when you check how well you have achieved the short-, medium- and long-term goals you set. Evaluate what you have achieved and look back at what went well and what went poorly.

MODERATED WORKSHOP LEARNING

Group discussion

Use the material presented in Chapter 4 as a launch pad for thinking about and critically discussing how the family approaches the balance between legacy and change in the business.

For the Current Gen, first prepare yourself, then discuss with the Next Gen:

> If the Next Gen proposed major changes to the legacy business, what concrete steps would you take to address their ideas?

For the Next Gen, first prepare yourself, then discuss with the Current Gen:

> If the Current Gen offered to join your efforts to change the existing business model/to develop a new business, how precisely would you involve them?

Case discussion

Read fictional case 4 and discuss the following questions:

> *Put yourself in the position of the uncles: what would it take to convince the uncles of the need for change?*
>
> *Put yourself in the position of the sixth gens: how can the sixth gens preserve the legacy and still drive change?*
>
> *As a consultant to the family, how would you advise uncles and sixth gens to take the business forward?*

Case simulation

Assume that one of the uncles travels to Singapore to meet his nephew who works as a Cheese Master in a luxury hotel. The two meet for lunch and exchange views on the future of Rose Cheese, now that one of Europe's leading cheese manufacturers has approached Rose to discuss taking it over.

For the Next Gen, assume the role of one of the uncles.

For the Current Gen, assume the role of the Next Gen who works as a Cheese Master in Singapore.

Starting positions: uncle makes the case for legacy and against change; sixth gen makes the case for legacy with change.

Those who are not involved in the simulation observe and comment.

Development plan for Current Gen/Next Gen

Draw up a development plan in which you define the following milestones:

Short term: What will I do by next week to close the legacy/change gap? What will I consider a success by then?

Medium term: What will I do by next month to close the legacy/change gap? What will I consider a success by then?

Long term: What will I do by next year to close the legacy/change gap? What will I consider a success by then?

Co-coaching

Choose a partner from a different generation and share your development plan with him or her. Arrange two follow-up meetings after two months and after six months to see how well you have implemented your plan.

CLASSROOM LEARNING

Group discussion

Use the material presented in Chapter 4 as a launch pad for thinking about and critically discussing how families approach the balance between legacy and change in the business.

Why does the Current Gen often value legacy over change?

What can be done to give the Next Gen the means to help transform the business?

Case discussion

Read fictional case 4 and discuss the following questions:

Put yourself in the position of the uncles: what would it take to convince the uncles of the need for change?

Put yourself in the position of the sixth gens: how can the sixth gens preserve the legacy and still drive change?

As a consultant to the family, how would you advise uncles and sixth gens to take the business forward?

Case simulation

Assume that one of the uncles travels to Singapore to meet his nephew who works as a Cheese Master in a luxury hotel. The two meet for lunch and exchange views on the future of Rose Cheese, now that one of Europe's leading cheese manufacturers has approached Rose to discuss taking it over.

Starting positions: uncle makes the case for legacy and against change; sixth gen makes the case for legacy with change.

Those who are not involved in the simulation observe and comment.

Oxford-style debate

Form two teams and prepare to debate the following thesis, with one team in favour and the other team against:

It needs the authority and credibility of the Current Gen to implement meaningful change in the family business.

Conduct a debate to collect all possible and valid arguments for and against the proposal.

Case report

Choose a family business that you know or are familiar with and analyse how well they have been able to balance legacy and change. Make concrete suggestions on how this alignment can be facilitated.

From practice vs theory to practice *and* theory

05

Review structure

CASE STUDY

Fictional case 5

She knew her father would never change.

Despite her warnings that their businesses needed time to consolidate, here he was about to sign yet another deal, in yet another country. France, no less! What did they know about France? The fundamental problem was that he couldn't relate to her way of thinking. She had school smarts, he had street smarts. On paper, he wanted to take advantage of her Harvard Business School education. In practice, he did as he pleased, expanding the family's business empire deal by far-flung deal. She was supposed to build the unifying structures that would hold his diverse ventures together, but, more than anything, she struggled to pin *him* down.

She respected his record. Thanks to her father's penchant for taking well-timed risks, a mid-sized Kolkata manufacturer of machine tools had successfully expanded into textiles and food processing, with subsidiaries and partnerships in Africa and all over the Middle East. What he didn't have in terms of formal education or international exposure, he made up for in charm, smarts and snap-of-the-fingers decisiveness.

Now on to France! It wasn't the size of the French deal that worried her, it was the pattern of her father's actions. Why did he tell her that he wanted to focus on ensuring long-term performance in the existing businesses, when in fact he could not help but run after every new opportunity that presented itself? It was exasperating.

When she confided in her closest friends from business school, themselves the children of entrepreneurs from Dubai and Singapore, she referred to her father's approach to business as 'just so old-fashioned' – intuitive, spontaneous and brilliant, but from a different world and less suited, perhaps, to maintaining a large, international firm. Having had similar experiences with their own fathers, they understood and commiserated.

'I get you, totally,' said Maha. 'My dad is just the same. It's just one project after another, like a game of poker, with hand after hand. Too many opportunities, not enough time!'

'Just do what you do best,' said Janice. 'He needs you to keep everything together, he just doesn't know it yet. One day, he'll thank you for insisting on doing things your way and putting some structure around the businesses.'

'I don't know. It's such a struggle sometimes. I mean, I get it, I understand why he's so good at what he does.'

As it was, her father left her a lot of freedom; as chief operating officer, she had initiated several quality improvement programmes and begun to implement firm-wide management systems. At least he didn't meddle, like so many other fathers she knew of. Having been persuaded to come home and help him run the business, she was looking for more: she wanted him to listen to her when it came to big questions about strategic positioning and long-term vision; she wanted him to take her seriously.

He was proud of his daughter. Harvard Business School, after all! Not to mention her stints in banking and consulting at well-known firms in New York and London. She wanted a bit of flair for the deal, true, she wasn't made in his likeness. For now, he expected her to learn from watching him in action – how to be quick, how to be shrewd, how to be tough. It would take some time on the job, but everything would fall into place. She was a good one. Already he could see that her efforts at cleaning up the company's computer systems were bearing fruit.

He knew she didn't like the French deal. What she couldn't understand, because he couldn't or wouldn't tell her, were his own, very personal reasons: the excitement of entering a new country, the pride about planting his very own flag in Europe and, probably most of all, the personal challenge. The truth was that he was getting bored and, having achieved far more than he had ever dreamed of, felt he needed to try something new.

On the spur of the moment, and although she had not been involved in working on the transaction up to that point, he decided to invite his daughter along for the last round of meetings prior to signing in Bordeaux. This would be a chance for her to see him in action. She was reluctant at first, because there was so much to do back home.

Quite apart from its fit with the rest of the family's activities, the French deal represented a unique challenge. There were multiple parties to the transaction; there were operations that needed to be streamlined against the opposition of local unions; and there were new investments to be made in modernizing equipment. She only knew the outline of the story and what she had been able to find out made it look like a very tall order.

The trip to France was a chance to be alone with her father, away from the hubbub of the rest of the family and the day-to-day distractions. On the plane, she hoped, he would open up to her about his long-term plans for the family business, beyond this deal. The Emirates flight to Paris left Kolkata in the morning and reached Paris in the evening. She would have more than a whole business day to grill him. He would have more than enough time to win her over.

'Why do you look so worried?'

'Why are you so confident that this is the right thing for us to do?'

She laid out her concerns in logical order. He had well-considered answers for each of her points, not in Business School vocabulary, but as a mix of experience and insight that was convincing to her. Where school had taught her to think in terms of economies of scale and learning curves, for example, he spoke of how the existing assembly process could be rejigged based on similar experience at home. Where she doubted revenue projections, he told a growth story based on individual resourcefulness and salesmanship. She admired her father's ability to dig deep down and get at the essentials: operations and people.

He found her questions sharpened his thinking and forced him to articulate what he would otherwise leave unsaid. Nobody in his inner circle dared to push him in the way she pushed him; his managers lacked the skill and his advisers lacked the will. He had all the answers, yes, but she was right to doubt the optimistic premises of the transaction. This thing was going to be a handful; there was a real danger that he would be drawn in and have to deal with much more than he had bargained for.

By the time the plane made its descent into Charles de Gaulle airport, she felt ready to sign – his arguments and optimism had once again carried the day. He, on the other hand, was not so sure anymore. Her reservations were well founded.

The next morning, at breakfast, he greeted her with that winning smile of his.

'I'm afraid we won't have the time for shopping today, my dear.'

'Why? Our train to Bordeaux doesn't leave until the afternoon.'

'Who's going to Bordeaux? Last night I got a new proposal – from Holland. Much more interesting for us, a bigger deal, something we can really get our teeth into. For this one, I will really be needing your help.'

'So, you didn't need me to do the Bordeaux deal, but now you do need me?'

'Forget Bordeaux! The train to Amsterdam leaves in two hours!'

The conceptual approach

The question of practice versus theory as it pertains to the family business is closely related to the question of legacy versus change, discussed in the preceding chapter. Formed by long years at the hot furnace of business, as it were, the Current Gen has a deeper sense of business practice than the Next Gen; conversely, the Next Gen frequently has a stronger grasp of business theory and economics, particularly of the newest thinking in these fields, picked up during studies and a variety of internships. This juxtaposition can lead the discussion about legacy and change to flounder for a lack of shared references. The Current Gen speaks from years of experience, both in markets and in processes; the Next Gen often argues from abstract principles or lessons learned from dissimilar cases. At a minimum, the juxtaposition of practice and theory can lead to misunderstanding and frustration. Both generations can express the feeling that the other does not understand and appreciate the value they bring to the table. When pushed, the Current Gen will revert to the impulse of protecting the legacy of the family business, while the Next Gen throws its hands up in frustration at the apparent impossibility of talking about change.

Understanding the juxtaposition of practice and theory in the family business

The question of practice versus theory is particularly relevant today. Up until the recent past, when the Next Gen still worked in the business from a very young age, the generations were similarly steeped in the practical know-how necessary to run the business: the Next Gen learned from their predecessors by following them around the factory. In an age when, for various reasons, family businesses do not involve the Next Gen as deeply from their early years and actively encourage higher study away from the business, with university education a mainstay of the Next Gen's personal development plans, this picture of the family business is increasingly out of date. In many families, the family business remains a central reference for the younger members, but their actual involvement is often only sporadic: there are too many other demands on their time. Ironically, the very academic learning that the Current Gen supports and pays for can contribute to the driving of a wedge between the generations. In some cases, Next Gens educated at university decide not to come home at all; those that do come back bring with them the excitement of new ideas and new attitudes. Especially when combined with further skill development outside of the family business, the hope of both generations may be that this learning serves to enrich and develop the family business. The reality is often different, as Current and Next Gens find that their approaches are not compatible, even if the Current Gen, in its time, also pursued higher studies. Many years of practical experience meet concentrated exposure to the newest methods, and perplexity results.

Before enumerating the differences of perspective between the generations that are shaped by the practice/theory divide, it is worth emphasizing that today's Next Gen is unlikely to be content being confined to a tightly circumscribed function, i.e. a job in a far-off factory or a position in the accounting department. As we have seen in the introduction, firm-level questions of strategy, sustainability and governance are of great interest to the Next Gen. Why does this Next Gen focus on the big picture? Broadly speaking, it has to do with access to information, education and socialization. In contrast to the relatively limited environment of their predecessor generations when they were young, this Next Gen is surrounded by information: everything is available to them, from environmental and societal trends to academic developments and, most importantly in our context, business success stories. They know what's going on and are quick to relate whatever they see and hear back to the family business. As outlined above, their education is also more likely to be broader and, in some cases, deeper than their predecessors'. Whether or not the Next Gen attends business school – many do – they will have had the opportunity to ask questions about business from many different angles, economics, statistics, information technology, public policy, etc., not only or even primarily from the point of view of a specialist preparing for a job in one profession. Socialization with the Next Gen of other business families, finally, plays the role of enriching a big-picture mindset. Brought together in various forums and keen to talk to each other of their own accord, today's Next Gen will have compared notes and discussed all kinds of ideas with their contemporaries from around the world. Even if they wanted to, they would have a very hard time explaining to their counterparts in other families why they had decided to accept a very narrow brief in the family business.

Practice versus theory and efforts to change the family business

The big picture of the Next Gen meets the Current Gen's experience of starting out in a tightly circumscribed and closely monitored specialist job. Unless the different starting points are understood, the generations are likely to clash over where and how the talents of the Next Gen are to be employed. Corporate purpose, governance, strategy, organization, technology, finance and human resources all enter into the equation when discussing how the perspectives of the Current and the Next Gen can run up against each other. Honed through years of on-the-job experience, the Current Gen is likely, at least initially, to take a sceptical view of the Next Gen's desire to roll up these types of questions. Some points, like purpose and governance, may seem too abstract and too far removed from everyday activity; others, such as strategy and organization, may seem premature in the light of the Next Gen's relative inexperience in the business; and operational topics in technology, finance and human resources may feel unduly threatening to the status quo, especially as these areas almost always involve non-family executives/managers and the Current Gen will be wary of allowing the Next Gen to interfere with the work of these key staff.

Beyond broad discussions of business purpose between the generations, the practice versus theory debate often crystallizes around concrete efforts to systematize the business. After all, much of management theory and best practice is about defining rules of success and putting in place systems for perpetuating efficient processes and routines. 'Making the business more professional' is the blanket phrase applied when proposing these kinds of changes. From their education and their experience in other cultures and businesses, the Next Gen will typically have a strong sense of what this means: detailed strategy plans, comprehensive management systems, well-endowed human resource functions, etc. From their long years in business practice, the Current Gen of family business leaders will often have a healthy sense of doubt about the everyday implications (and costs!) of this phrase. Particularly in businesses that rely heavily on the Current Gen's ability to build personal relationships and make deals in difficult markets, so-called professionalization can be seen as irrelevant or, worse, constraining the leaders' freedom to act. Think about the case of the emerging markets entrepreneur whose very success is based on the ability to make deals that break the boundaries of every business handbook: unstable political environments, doubtful counterparties and underdeveloped yet complex markets. Theory would say 'Hands off', but practical experience makes deals such as these appear as a calculable risk for the entrepreneur. How to explain this brand of practical smarts to the well-schooled Next Gen? How to teach them to become deal-makers in their turn? Correspondingly, how to make the Current Gen deal-maker understand that, in the long run, the family business would surely benefit from incorporating the newest approaches to professionalization and systematization?

Taking an ethnographic approach to learning by doing

Practice and theory are unequal twins. In the social sciences, and in the humanities more generally, the practice versus theory debate goes back a long way. In his *Nicomachean Ethics*, Aristotle distinguished between *phronesis* (practical wisdom) and *sophia* (theoretical wisdom), and argued that both are necessary for understanding how the world works.[1] A focus on practice, and the particular experience, limits generalizability; general theory, on the other hand, like any form of abstraction, obscures some aspects of a problem while illuminating others. Where businesses rely on successful practices rooted in their specific context, universities stress theoretical approaches that lay claim to general validity: practice vs theory, the specific vs the general.

This split is mirrored in many family businesses, particularly in discussions between hands-on Current Gens and Next Gens fresh out of university or stints in finance and consulting. Even in academia, however, recent years have seen a considerable amount of effort spent on bridging the gap between practice and theory. Inspired by the work of Bourdieu and Foucault among others, contemporary researchers in sociology and the philosophy of science such as Schatzki have argued for a turn to what they call 'practice theory', i.e. theory that is grounded in and reflects the changing nature of actual practice.[2] In other words, theory needs to meet the test of practice, just as much as practice needs to meet the test of theory. This movement of combining practice and theory has spread across the social sciences, including the fields of management and organization and has encouraged deeper study of how social units and individual actors of the most diverse types *actually perform* in context and over time.[3] Actual performance, in turn, is exactly what business is based upon.

While we do not expect family businesses to adopt social science research methods, some aspects of this approach to resolving apparently unbridgeable differences between practice and theory may be worth emulating. In particular, taking the ethnographic approach of full immersion in the day-to-day life of the subject matter for tackling hard-to-quantify but essential savoir-faire such as, for example, deal making skills or customer relations competences could help strengthen mutual understanding.[4] What is the ethnographic approach, and how does it differ from good old learning on the job or even apprenticeship? Take deal-making skills, that is, scouting, negotiating and completing a new venture, be it an investment, a partnership, or even an acquisition: traditionally, the Current Gen would take the Next Gen along for the ride to observe how deals are put together and point out pitfalls to avoid along the way. Indeed, this is still what happens in many family businesses today. The ethnographic approach builds on the traditional model, requiring of both generations that they actively reflect on what they are doing and learning. Active reflection usually involves a combination of taking notes, putting together written accounts, consulting the relevant research literature and discussing the findings with a variety of people to deepen understanding. The effects of learning by doing are thus augmented; learning becomes an observable output of the process and involves both generations. Explicit focus on learning has the additional benefit of defusing disagreement over practice versus theory. Instead of getting caught up in polarizing debates about what this process or that process should look like,

Current and Next Gens spend more time together observing and accounting for what the business actually does.

Integrating practice and theory

Different family businesses are at different stages of development and sophistication, of course, but, in most cases, it is unlikely that the Next Gen's demands for the most advanced ways of doing things will be fully satisfied by the existing organization. In founder-led businesses and in family businesses based in emerging markets, the contrasts between practice and theory can be particularly striking, as Current Gen entrepreneurs who are used to doing whatever it takes to succeed (the famous 'shirtsleeves' approach) confront Next Gen graduates advocating approaches drawing upon (international) best practice. Part of the disagreement comes from the fact that international best practices are largely based on studies carried out and experiences made in advanced markets, particularly the United States and Europe, where many if not all of the Next Gen will have gone for advanced education and/or further seasoning. What is essential for a business to succeed in an advanced market is not necessarily the same in an emerging market. Conversely, what works in an emerging market may not be applicable in an advanced market. In other words, the gap between practice and theory that separates the Current Gen from the Next Gen is also context specific. The larger the difference between markets, the more pronounced the gap.

Transformation initiatives in strategy, sustainability or governance, such as the ones discussed in the introduction to this book and taken up again in Chapter 11, represent a particularly challenging but also a fertile ground for addressing and ultimately overcoming the juxtaposition of practice versus theory. In many cases, not all, the impetus for a transformation initiative arises from the Next Gen's desire to apply to the core operation of the family business what they have learned at university and in first jobs with other companies. Thus, new business models to outflank the competition, supply chain reorganizations to meet sustainability objectives, or revised family governance frameworks to prepare for leadership succession might be presented to the Current Gen as theoretically desirable and necessary improvements to the way the family does business. Revolutionary ideas meet well-established ways of working and the practice versus theory gap looms large. More often than not, the Current Gen dismisses the Next Gen's ideas as impractical and impracticable, while the Next Gen decries their elders' unwillingness to accept new concepts from outside their immediate sphere of lived know-how. In order to avoid debilitating conflict in cases like these, it is important to acknowledge that successful transformation initiatives require both practice and theory, both the Current Gen's experience and the Next Gen's courage to try what is new and untested in the context of the family business.

More generally, the gap between practice and theory in family businesses can be seen as an opportunity to take a long look at the business and come up with ideas for change. Once precisely assessed, the appraisal of concrete gaps between practice and theory can give rise to productive, goal-oriented improvement programs: not practice versus theory, but practice *and* theory. In the best case, both generations recognize that they need each other's distinct skills. In contrast to the traditional, hierarchical picture of family business that depicts the older generation as the teachers and the younger generation as the students, it is more useful to think about the process of building deep understanding as one of reciprocal development. Why can't both generations act as both teachers and students? Much as in addressing the questions of legacy and change described in Chapter 4, trust maturity between the generations is a prerequisite for this kind of exchange. Deep down, the Current Gen and the Next Gen often admire each other for their respective capabilities, the Current Gen amazed at the Next Gen's easy grasp of new concepts and new technologies, and the Next Gen highly respectful of the Current Gen's track record and leadership acumen. The tensions between them arise from difficulties in communicating openly (Chapter 1), making implicit feelings of obligation explicit (Chapter 2) and overcoming archetypal conflicts (Chapter 3).

KEY TAKEAWAYS

1. Different generations may clash over the relative importance of practice and theory.
2. Gaps between practice and theory provide opportunities for rethinking the business.
3. Transformation initiatives can serve as vehicles for implementing fresh concepts.

Learning journey: Pit stop 5

Please refer to Chapter 12 for a full explanation of the educational approach supporting the learning journey.

SELF-LEARNING

Self-assessment

Assess where you and the other generation are and should be on the continuum between practice vs theory and practice and *theory.*

Self-reflection

Current Gen: Think through the following statements. How true are they of your own situation?

Practical experience and theoretical learning get equal treatment in our business.

The Next Gen does not give enough weight to practical experience.

The Next Gen is often naïve about the application of theory.

Next Gen: Think through the following statements. How true are they of your own situation?

Practical experience and theoretical learning get equal treatment in our business.

The Current Gen sometimes gives too much weight to practical experience.

The Current Gen is often dismissive about the application of theory.

Development plan for Current Gen/Next Gen

Draw up a development plan in which you define the following milestones:

Short term: What will I do by next week to close the practice/theory gap? What will I consider a success by then?

Medium term: What will I do by next month to close the practice/theory gap? What will I consider a success by then?

Long term: What will I do by next year to close the practice/theory gap? What will I consider a success by then?

Action review

Mark the dates in your calendar when you check how well you have achieved the short-, medium- and long-term goals you set. Evaluate what you have achieved and look back at what went well and what went poorly.

MODERATED WORKSHOP LEARNING

Group discussion

Use the material presented in Chapter 5 as a launch pad for thinking about and critically discussing how the family approaches the balance between practice and theory in the business.

For the Current Gen, first prepare yourself, then discuss with the Next Gen:

> How do you/can you incorporate the fresh skills of the Next Gen in growing the family business?

For the Next Gen, first prepare yourself, then discuss with the Current Gen:

> How do you/can you incorporate the accumulated skills of the Current Gen in working on your own ideas for the family business?

Case discussion

Read fictional case 5 and discuss the following questions:

> *Put yourself in the position of the father: what can the father learn from the daughter? How best to do so?*
>
> *Put yourself in the position of the daughter: what can the daughter learn from the father? How best to do so?*
>
> *As a consultant to the family, how would you advise father and daughter to go about learning from each other?*

Case simulation

Replay the conversation about the French deal between the daughter and her father in your own words.

For the Next Gen, assume the role of the father.

For the Current Gen, assume the role of the daughter.

Starting positions: father explains what makes him successful; daughter explains how the business can be made better.

Those who are not involved in the simulation observe and comment.

Development plan for Current Gen/Next Gen

Draw up a development plan in which you define the following milestones:

Short term: What will I do by next week to close the practice/theory gap? What will I consider a success by then?

Medium term: What will I do by next month to close the practice/theory gap? What will I consider a success by then?

Long term: What will I do by next year to close the practice/theory gap? What will I consider a success by then?

Co-coaching

Choose a partner from a different generation and share your development plan with him or her. Arrange two follow-up meetings after two months and after six months to see how well you have implemented your plan.

CLASSROOM LEARNING

Group discussion

Use the material presented in Chapter 5 as a launch pad for thinking about and critically discussing how families approach the balance between practice and theory in the business.

Why do practice and theory often collide in intergenerational relationships in the family business context?

Case discussion

Read fictional case 5 and discuss the following questions:

Put yourself in the position of the father: what can the father learn from the daughter? How best to do so?

Put yourself in the position of the daughter: what can the daughter learn from the father? How best to do so?

As a consultant to the family, how would you advise father and daughter to go about learning from each other?

Case simulation

Replay the conversation about the French deal between the daughter and her father in your own words.

Starting positions: father explains what makes him successful; daughter explains how the business can be made better.

Those who are not involved in the simulation observe and comment.

Oxford-style debate

Form two teams and prepare to debate the following thesis, with one team in favour and the other team against:

> Practice always beats theory, a lesson that the Next Gen will learn when they have gained sufficient experience.

Conduct a debate to collect all possible and valid arguments for and against the proposal.

Case report

Choose a family business that you know or are familiar with and analyse how they are able to value both practice and theory in shaping the future of the family business. Make concrete suggestions on how this balance can be further improved.

From internal vs external to internal *and* external

06

Rethink practices

CASE STUDY

Fictional case 6

His ancestors had founded the bank in Aleppo during the Silk Road's heyday and Sabah was the 11th Grazi to head the family firm. Unlike their contemporary rivals, the Grazis eschewed growth and prized safety. As a result, the bank never diversified significantly, staying close to the confidential needs of the merchant families it had been created to serve. Sabah left Aleppo as a child and the Next Gen of Grazis were all born in Geneva, where the extended family settled, obtained a banking licence and carried on the tradition of working with wealthy clients from the Middle East. In the rapidly changing landscape of 21st century private banking, Banque Grazi was one of the lone constants, emphasizing deep knowledge of the client and highly personalized service.

The world evolved, Banque Grazi remained constant. Sabah Grazi personally welcomed important clients with rich, sweet coffee and familiar questions about their parents as well as their children. Elegant in a discreet way, Sabah wore dark blue suits and crisp white shirts; never did he venture to try a smart-casual look; never did he splash on too much cologne; never did he lose his composure. From the way he carried himself to the way he spoke in measured, self-assured tones, everything about

Sabah Grazi exuded solidity and reliability. Sabah was Banque Grazi and Banque Grazi was Sabah.

First-born son André was Sabah's pride. André combined the abstract intellect of his mother's family with the commercial acumen of the Grazi's and, at the young age of 28, had already founded a successful business. Not only had he been able to raise outside funding, he had also entered into development alliances with several global software companies. Although André looked and dressed the part of a 'tech bro', he was not a stereotypical tech entrepreneur. For him, software was a means to an end, not some kind of higher calling to change the world. Running his own business gave him the freedom to be himself, to live his life exactly as he pleased. Sabah observed André's achievements with a smile in one eye and a tear in the other. If only André's brilliance could be harnessed for the benefit of the family firm!

As long as information technology played no significant role in the development of the bank, there was no chance of attracting or even interesting André. He appreciated the history of the firm and understood what it meant to be a Grazi, but he could not see himself working with his father in traditional private banking. Fortunately for André, there were enough other younger Grazis around, including his brother and sister who had already started their careers in finance. As much as his father may have wanted André to follow in his footsteps, the question of his entering the firm had never gone past the stage of a long look in his direction at family gatherings.

Then, one day, by himself and after months of reflection, Sabah decided that the time had finally come for the bank to digitize its operations. He had resisted modernity for long enough and the tide could not be held back anymore. From every point of view – government regulation, risk evaluation, customer relationship administration and cost management – digitization offered benefits that were necessary if the bank was going to continue on its centuries-long journey. Indeed, and this is what had made Sabah's mind up, even the most traditional clients were starting to ask for digital access. Sabah recognized the enormity of the task; he also knew where to look for help with this critical project. Who better than André, Sabah asked himself? Who else could he trust with such a delicate and vital mission?

Getting André on board would not be simple. His relationship with the family business was one of affection rather than interest; he had never wanted to work in the bank; he already had his own successful company.

Sabah was well aware of all this, but pressed forward regardless, making André an offer so enticing that it would be difficult for the younger Grazi to refuse: a combination of flattery, incentive, guilt and freedom to implement the best technology as he saw fit. Even dressed up in such an alluring package, it was very hard to convince the younger Grazi to take time away from his own business to help the family firm. Something André had always resisted was now coming back to haunt him: was there no way for a Grazi to escape Banque Grazi? Sabah pulled all the strings. What finally made the difference in the project's favour for André was the well-argued intervention of his mother: concise, practical and reassuring. Specifications and deadlines were his to define; resources were no object; most saliently, the digitization of Banque Grazi was a limited and manageable commitment of André's energies.

Thrilled as he was with the outcome of the deliberations with André, Sabah was also apprehensive about the security implications of the project. Digitization meant making information concerning the bank's operations more broadly available than it had ever been before, internally and, potentially, externally. The last thing he wanted to do was to put the bank's gold-plated reputation for discretion on the line. What if, God forbid, sensitive information somehow leaked out? The possible consequences were too frightening to even think about. Accordingly, Sabah made maintaining secrecy about clients a critical success factor of the system implementation, impressing upon André how damaging it would be to the Grazi name if digitization led to information leaks, client misidentifications, or any other similar embarrassments. André understood his father's concerns and did his best to alleviate them. He promised that the work would be done not only efficiently, but also safely.

Once the project got under way, Sabah backed off and gave André the free hand he had promised, including authority over how to spend the budgeted funds. He knew he was out of his depth and, after working so hard to lure André back into the fold, he didn't want to risk irritating him with a layman's questions. True to his word, André put the day-to-day operations of the software business he had co-founded in the hands of one of his partners and focused his attention on the Banque Grazi digitization project, drawing on a small cadre of his own company's software engineers for help with the most critical elements and lining up partnerships with SAP and PwC for some of the heavy lifting behind the scenes that a project like this inevitably entailed.

André knew that his father would object to the idea of working with partners from outside the family's immediate personal orbit. To avoid interminable emotional debates, he decided not to tell him about the involvement of the software house and the implementation specialist. It wasn't that André disrespected his father's concerns about privacy; it was just that he didn't think they would be relevant in this context. The outside firms would not get access to any sensitive client information and, in any case, their reputations also rested on maintaining data security. You shared what you needed to share in order to get the job done. That was how the business of system implementation worked.

On time, on budget and fully functional; after just nine months André delivered on all counts and Sabah was thrilled with the results, so thrilled that he let down his guard. Once a quarter, a select group of Geneva private bankers rented the dignified rooms of the Cercle de la Terrasse for a casual meeting of the minds. Sabah felt comfortable in these surroundings and with these people. To a select few, in a circle of three and well out of the larger group's hearing, he opened up about the digitization project at Banque Grazi – more than anything else, to be able to share his pride in André's accomplishment.

'Welcome to the 21st century,' said Jean-Marc, a principal at one of Geneva's oldest banking houses.

'I never thought you would take the plunge,' offered Pierre, Chairman Emeritus of the Geneva Bankers' Association. 'I heard from a friend of a friend that PwC was on the job, too. Would you recommend them for the digitization work we are planning at my foundation?'

'PwC?' echoed Sabah, as he summoned up a lifetime of self-control to maintain his poise. 'Oh, yes, of course, PwC; yes, they know what they are doing.'

The conceptual approach

The juxtapositions of legacy vs change, practice vs theory and internal vs external place the Current and the Next Gens at opposite ends of three distinct categories of thinking. These juxtapositions can either reinforce a hierarchical mindset between the generations, or, if resolved by mutual appreciation, stimulate effective intergenerational collaboration. The internal vs external juxtaposition – that is, the observation that the Current

Gen will generally prefer internal solutions to questions arising in the business whereas the Next Gen will be agnostic about the source of know-how and actively seek out external solutions – is especially relevant for thinking about innovation and change. It is another generation gap, in other words, but this is an especially important one, with much broader implications than are commonly acknowledged. Indeed, if the Current Gen and the Next Gen do not learn how to work together effectively to open up the family business so that it can take full advantage of skills and resources from outside the organization to drive change and innovation, they may be putting the very future of the family business at risk.

Understanding openness

The Next Gen has grown up in a social and economic context that favours openness towards the outside world in everything from the personal to the technological; in particular, the ubiquity of social media has encouraged the sharing of very personal information, while the existence of open exchange platforms on the internet for software development, academic research and, most recently, artificial intelligence, has made technology-sharing a new norm. There are internet interest groups for everything: accordingly, members of the Next Gen have also formed numerous formal and informal associations, across borders, across business categories and across families. To put it simply, the Next Gen regard it as self-evident that important questions be discussed with outsiders and outside solutions be adopted whenever appropriate.

By contrast, the Current Gen of family business leaders are often sceptical about dealing with outsiders, both in sharing information and in making use of what is not developed in house. On the one hand, the Current Gen did not grow up with social media and hence does not have the same level of comfort as the Next Gen in openly exchanging information, personal or otherwise. On the other hand, an aversion to risk, manifested by a desire to protect the family formula, figures as an enduring characteristic of family businesses, imprinted on past generations from a very young age. On top of business risk aversion, family businesses have traditionally always been very concerned with reputational risk, particularly the risk that personal failings of individuals might pose to the business. Taken together, these factors tend to make the Current Gen wary of opening up to outsiders.

The divergence in perspectives about sharing information and working with information from the outside creates a significant barrier between the generations when it comes to discussing whether or not to work with external partners in taking the family business forward into new markets and new ways of doing things. The Next Gen will be full of ideas of where to find and how to tap external sources, while the Current Gen will want to put the brakes on opening up, in some cases even formulating strict rules about how representatives of the family business are to interact with the outside world. Instead of being enriching for the family business, the fundamental difference in attitudes to internal and external sources often becomes a strong bone of contention between Current and Next Gens.

Recall from Chapter 4 and W Brian Arthur that new technologies arise out of (new) combinations of existing technologies. Indeed, this statement describes how most, if not all (family) businesses got started: an entrepreneur or a team of entrepreneurs see the possibility of meeting a new need or an existing need in a new way by drawing on all technological possibilities available to them, from inside *and* from outside the confines of their firm. Business founders, in general, have no alternative to scrapping for any input, internal or external; they cannot be choosy about where their ideas come from. In a sense, therefore, the emphasis the Next Gen puts on looking outside for ideas and resources represents a return to the start-up mindset of the founders. Like the founders in their own time, members of the Next Gen are not afraid to scout their surroundings and appropriate for their own use whatever seems to work; like the founders also, they are willing to open up about what they need and, in so doing, share what they know. Thanks to modern technology and the spirit of openness that characterizes their generation, the whole world is at their fingertips and they cannot imagine being limited to what is in-house.

Openness to external know-how and innovation

How does openness to external know-how contribute to innovation and change, and ultimately lead to improved business performance? Open innovation, the concept made popular by Chesbrough and others, reveals the limitations of relying only on internal ideas and technologies for innovation and legitimizes a broader, source neutral search for the best in the effort of businesses to adapt and grow.[1] The basic reasoning behind open innovation is straightforward: given the speed and breadth of technological development in the 21st century, no one company can possibly own all of the knowledge resources necessary to keep up. Therefore, if a business is to continue to innovate, collaboration with outside sources becomes a competitive necessity. The reasoning behind open innovation may be straightforward, but the implementation is not. Collaboration with outside sources requires new forms of organization – joint ventures, strategic alliances, even agreements about competitive networks – and new management approaches. Moreover, and this is critical, these new forms and new approaches concern innovation that affects not just peripheral activities that can be simply outsourced or shared without much further thought, but the very heart of the business. Chesbrough and others have demonstrated convincingly that open innovation works. Not only does it work, it has become the standard modus operandi in numerous sectors where continuous innovation is critical: information and internet software, communications hardware and pharmaceuticals, to name the most prominent. Success stories are many. Indeed, one-time start-ups like NVIDIA or ARM and others like them have based their rise to prominence in considerable measure on open innovation methods.

What does the now well-established trend towards open innovation mean for family businesses? Ironically, sending the young away for a period of time, to learn from related firms and friendly business partners, represents one of the traditional tenets of developing Next Gen leaders. However, going away to be seasoned is not the same thing as approaching every problem, including problems that are central to the strategy and governance of the family business, with an openness to external perspectives. In the traditional career model for the Next Gen, openness to the outside ends with the completion of the Next Gen's apprenticeship; today's Next Gen continues to seek know-how from the outside, even once they have returned to the family business. As discussed above, sharing information with and building on the ideas of outsiders is a way of life for them. They will not stop using social media, forming interest groups with like-minded individuals and talking about their business and their family with others who have something to say about the subject just because they have formally (re-)entered the family business.

Secrecy and control

While the Next Gen's openness fits well with the management philosophy of open innovation that prevails in many industries today, it flies in the face of several long-established family business norms, most notably *secrecy* and *control*. As sketched out above, Current Gen leaders will have been taught to maintain a strict silence about the internal workings of the business and the family when interacting with outsiders.[2] If anything of substance is to be revealed, it is only to related parties like lawyers, long-term and select friends who have earned the trust of the family over years of loyal service. Such a habit of secrecy can prevent the family business from engaging in the kind of open exchange with outsiders, especially freshly made contacts, that the Next Gen takes for granted. If and when the family business does decide to appropriate outside know-how, it is common practice to seek control of that know-how, typically through acquisition. Rather than working with a network of alliances, joint ventures and other loose forms of partnership, as is increasingly common in an economy of open innovation, the family business generally prefers to own the know-how.[3] In other words, the juxtaposition between internal and external is more than a difference between the generations: it goes to the heart of how the family business conceives of itself.

As mentioned in Chapter 4, many family businesses are active in capital-intensive and relationship-focused industries. It is fair to say that openness to externally sourced know-how and the accompanying change of innovation culture have come to these industries only relatively recently, many years after high-tech and pharmaceuticals opened the floodgates to open innovation and external cooperation. As long as change was slow and competitive advantage protected, the need to engage in the new practice of working with external partners to innovate was limited. The known values of secrecy and control trumped the unproven potential of external idea sourcing and partnering. The question is – how many family businesses can still count on things staying this way, slow to change and protected from competition? The first twenty plus years of the 21st century have proven that rapid, dramatic change can come to any industry and that competitive advantage is increasingly short-lived.[4] This is also the experience that the Next Gen has grown up with and uses as a reference for its thinking. Even if the family business is not in high tech, the Next Gen may be convinced that it can benefit from the high-tech type of approach to drawing upon external know-how for innovation and change.

Integrating external and internal: When to be open and when to be closed

The traditional preferences for secrecy and control still have relevance in the family business. Secrecy about ownership arrangements and about family disagreements helps the family to maintain a united front vis-à-vis employees and other stakeholders. Control of the means of production ensures that what makes the family business distinctive extends to all of its operations. However, secrecy and control do not need to be seen as blanket commandments. Given the spread of information in social media and elsewhere, it is not possible to maintain absolute secrecy anyway, and families are forced to think about what exactly should remain secret under all circumstances and what can be allowed into the open. Some families, particularly those active in industries like food or medicine that touch large parts of the population, have found that it is actually helpful for the reputation of the family to share some information. In that way, the consumer/citizen can feel more confident in the product and who stands behind it. In terms of business secrets, it is important to weigh the advantages and the disadvantages of keeping quiet. Some business secrets are in fact not secret anymore, despite the family's best efforts, while other closely guarded processes might in fact benefit from exposure to new ideas from the outside. Control in the sense of maintaining one hundred per cent ownership is also not always necessary, not from the point of view of family uniqueness and not from the point of view of having the final say. As open innovation and the accompanying exposure to new hybrid forms of organization become more common, suppliers and customers of the family business begin to expect that it will open up more and try different ways of working together. Again, it is a question of adapting – to the times and to the situation. Control, like secrecy, is not an end in itself.

Opening up to external know-how – drawing upon the best of what is out there and sharing what you can share – has become a competitive necessity for every business and hence also for family businesses. The degree of openness is best adapted to the specific context, with different families experimenting with and settling on different approaches. Open innovation takes time to get good at, multiple partnerships, many ups and downs, and a lot of learning along the way. It is important to stress that organizing for open innovation is different from setting up a partnership here and there, i.e.

for the purposes of market access in foreign countries. It involves a fundamental rethink about how to deal with intellectual capital, how to address the family business's needs for secrecy and control. Secrecy and control will remain as important precepts of the family business, but as principles to be respected, not as unquestioned rules. Again, this is an area where the family business can benefit from and/and or win/win thinking between the generations. In the ideal case, the implementation of openness to external know-how is a matter of intergenerational consultation, with the Current Gen learning from the Next Gen about the newest best practices from research and unfamiliar industrial experience, and the Next Gen drawing upon the Current Gen's feel for how to keep the family united and preserve the values of the business. As much as, if not more than other recent external challenges the family business has faced – strategic from bigger competitors, financial in terms of access to capital and regulatory to open the books – organizing for open innovation calls for a re-invention of how the family business conceives of itself. In this process, the Current Gen can learn a lot from how the Next Gen works with potential partners; conversely, the Next Gen can absorb a great deal from the Current Gen when it comes to preserving the essence of the family business.

KEY TAKEAWAYS

1. Current Gens and New Gens differ in their views about the suitability of business openness.
2. Business openness to external knowledge sources is a primary driver of innovation.
3. Openness can be managed with respect for what makes the family business unique.

Learning journey: Pit stop 6

Please refer to Chapter 12 for a full explanation of the educational approach supporting the learning journey.

SELF-LEARNING

Self-assessment

Assess where you and the other generation are and should be on the continuum between internal vs external and internal and *external.*

Self-reflection

Current Gen: Think through the following statements. How true are they of your own situation?

Innovation comes from inside the business.

Our business is quite open to partnerships for innovation.

For our existing partnerships, we have clear objectives in place.

Next Gen: Think through the following statements. How true are they of your own situation?

Innovation comes from inside the business.

Our business is not very open to partnerships for innovation.

For our existing partnerships, the objectives in place need to be clarified.

Development plan for Current Gen/Next Gen

Draw up a development plan in which you define the following milestones:

Short term: What will I do by next week to close the internal/external gap? What will I consider a success by then?

Medium term: What will I do by next month to close the internal/external gap? What will I consider a success by then?

Long term: What will I do by next year to close the internal/external gap? What will I consider a success by then?

Action review

Mark the dates in your calendar when you check how well you have achieved the short-, medium- and long-term goals you set. Evaluate what you have achieved and look back at what went well and what went poorly.

MODERATED WORKSHOP LEARNING

Group discussion

Use the material presented in Chapter 6 as a launch pad for thinking about and critically discussing how the family approaches the balance between internal and external inputs in developing the business.

For the Current Gen, first prepare yourself, then discuss with the Next Gen:

How could innovation in the family business benefit from new alliances, knowledge partnerships and co-marketing agreements?

For the Next Gen, first prepare yourself, then discuss with the Current Gen:

What risks should the family business be concerned about with new alliances, knowledge partnerships and co-marketing agreements?

Case discussion

Read fictional case 6 and discuss the following questions:

Put yourself in the position of Sabah: why is Sabah against external help? In what ways is he right/wrong?

Put yourself in the position of André: why does André defy Sabah's wishes? In what ways is he right/wrong?

As a consultant to the family, how would you advise Sabah and André to mend fences and move on?

Case simulation

Replay the conversation between the son and his father in your own words.

For the Next Gen, assume the role of the father.

For the Current Gen, assume the role of the son.

Starting positions: Sabah confronts André over his betrayal of trust; André argues for efficiency gains from partnership.

Those who are not involved in the simulation observe and comment.

Development plan for Current Gen/Next Gen

Draw up a development plan in which you define the following milestones:

Short term: What will I do by next week to close the internal/external gap? What will I consider a success by then?

Medium term: What will I do by next month to close the internal/external gap? What will I consider a success by then?

Long term: What will I do by next year to close the internal/external gap? What will I consider a success by then?

Co-coaching

Choose a partner from a different generation and share your development plan with him or her. Arrange two follow-up meetings after two months and after six months to see how well you have implemented your plan.

CLASSROOM LEARNING

Group discussion

Use the material presented in Chapter 6 as a launch pad for thinking about and critically discussing how families approach the balance between internal and external inputs in developing the business.

Why might the Current Gen be critical of external inputs?

What conditions facilitate a balanced use of internal and external development inputs in the family business?

Case discussion

Read fictional case 6 and discuss the following questions:

Put yourself in the position of Sabah: why is Sabah against external help? In what ways is he right/wrong?

Put yourself in the position of André: why does André defy Sabah's wishes? In what ways is he right/wrong?

As a consultant to the family, how would you advise Sabah and André to mend fences and move on?

Case simulation

Replay the conversation between the son and his father in your own words.

Starting positions: Sabah confronts André over his betrayal of trust; André argues for efficiency gains from partnership.

Those who are not involved in the simulation observe and comment.

Oxford-style debate

Form two teams and prepare to debate the following thesis, with one team in favour and the other team against:

> The Next Gen can only succeed in the family business if they demonstrate an appreciation for the company's current internal capabilities.

Conduct a debate to collect all possible and valid arguments for and against the proposal.

Case report

Choose a family business that you know or are familiar with and analyse how they manage the balance between internal and external inputs in developing the business. Make concrete suggestions on how this balance can be fostered.

PART THREE
Role respect
Governance processes

Meantime, we shall express our darker purpose.
Give me the map there. Know we have divided
In three our kingdom; and 'tis our fast intent
To shake all cares and business from our age,
Conferring them on younger strengths while we
Unburthen'd crawl toward death. Our son of Cornwall
And you, our no less loving son of Albany,
We have this hour a constant will to publish
Our daughters' several dowers, that future strife
May be prevented now. The Princes, France and Burgundy,
Great rivals in our youngest daughter's love,
Long in our court have made their amorous sojourn,
And here are to be answer'd. Tell me, my daughters
(Since now we will divest us both of rule,
Interest of territory, cares of state)
Which of you shall we say doth love us most?
That we our largest bounty may extend
Where nature doth with merit challenge. Goneril,
Our eldest-born, speak first.

WILLIAM SHAKESPEARE, *KING LEAR*, ACT I, SCENE 1

King Lear remains the quintessential succession drama, and no book about or popular treatment of succession would be complete without reference to Lear's ill-fated attempt to divide his kingdom among his daughters, in direct proportion to their love ('Which of you shall we say doth love us most? That we our largest bounty may extend…'). *King Lear* is not the only one of the great tragedies to address succession: *Macbeth*, *Hamlet* and *Julius Caesar* also focus on the passage of supreme power.[1] What these tragedies have in common with each other and with the contemporary reality of Elizabethan England is the absence of a well-defined and broadly agreed upon *governance process* for regulating succession. Succession is up for grabs and arbitrary, with the protagonists making up the rules as they go along. Not surprisingly, therefore, Shakespeare's treatments of succession involve intense personal rivalry and invariably lead to armed conflict and societal upheaval. In short, *King Lear* and the other succession dramas, while they have a lot to teach us about human ambition in the quest for power, do not speak to the question of how the succession process can be governed. On the contrary, they provide a blueprint of what *not* to do.

Every family business contains the seeds of a Shakespearean drama. Even where trust between the generations has matured and differing capabilities are appreciated, there may be significant conflict over roles. Typically, the Current Gen is still firmly in charge, but the Next Gen is trying to establish its position, and the inherent imbalance of power can get in the way of effective collaboration. Both generations feel a strong sense of responsibility towards the business and each may think that it alone knows what is best for the future. As a consequence, the older generation holds on to the helm for longer than it otherwise would have, while the younger generation pushes to take charge earlier. How to take (some of) the drama out of generational transition and foster an approach rooted in the side-by-side mindset? *Role respect* becomes the watchword for both generations, as they work together to build and/or reinforce the governance process related to succession. Both the Current and the Next Gens have a specific role to play in the life of the family business, the current as a guarantor of stability, the next as a catalyst for the future. In practice, different views of time are often a primary source of conflict over roles, with an attitude of 'Wait your turn' set against an attitude of 'I'm ready now', and both generations failing to respect each other's distinct positions in the long-term evolution of the family business (Chapter 7). Role-related issues can amplify differences between the generations over when to share power, particularly where the governance of the family business is still loosely defined or poorly implemented (Chapter 8). Considerations of time and power often come to a head around the topic of leadership succession in the family business (Chapter 9).

Learning approach: Side by side as governance process

What is unique about corporate governance in the family business? Apart from adhering to the standards required for legal incorporation and ensuring compliance with the standards of accounting necessary to satisfy suppliers, banks and regulators, the family business can define corporate governance any way it likes. Unless legally required to do so, as is the case in some jurisdictions, the family business does not have to appoint a board of directors, nor does it have to spell out a shareholder's agreement or a leadership succession plan. The family business does not have to have corporate governance and therefore many don't bother. After all, corporate governance and everything that goes with it – documents, committees, meetings, compliance procedures, etc. – represents a cost. In addition, the benefits are hard to measure and the time invested in governance takes away from the time spent selling more widgets. As a result of this inattention to corporate governance, too many family businesses are predestined to experience their own King Lear moment. Thinking about generational transition in the terms presented in this book puts the topic of governance at the top of the family business agenda. Side by side is not sustainable without a working governance process.

- **Point of departure**

  → *Corporate governance is about creating a dynamic balance of powers.* The purpose of corporate governance is to ensure the long-term viability of the corporation. If effective corporate governance is in place, no single individual or decision-making body has unchecked power, and the critical numbers are put together in such a way that accountability is guaranteed.[2] Accordingly, corporate governance is not just about having a structure. In fact, thinking about corporate governance as a rigid structure can be source of trouble, if underlying business conditions undergo significant change. Much more appropriate, then, to think of corporate governance in the family business as a process that leads to a structure and also contains the seeds of change. If corporate governance is a process, it can evolve with the business and with the people.

- **Important assumptions**

  → *A balance of powers is better, in the long run, for sustaining the (family) business.* Here, too, as in the case of the discussion of trust maturity in Part One (side by side as social psychology), we have the age-old question about the relative merits of dominant, top-down decision-making vs balanced powers. From a governance perspective, there can be times in the life of an organization when dominant decision-making is preferable (see Chapter 8 for more detail on the conditions); however, the risk with dominant decision-making is that it becomes entrenched, serves the interests of the individual(s) in power and ultimately undermines the business. It follows that smooth generational transition is impeded by an imbalance of powers and a lack of effective corporate governance.

- **Normative implications**

  → *Build a corporate governance process and structure that serves multiple generations.* For those family businesses that do not have any corporate governance to speak of, generational transition represents an opportunity to go to the drawing board and work out processes and structures that are agreed upon by both the Current and the Next Gens. Indeed, this is precisely the objective of the governance initiatives we describe in Chapters 1 and 11. For families that do have a working corporate governance framework, the imminent entry of the Next Gen into the existing institutions of governance (ownership committee, board of directors or executive team) offers the chance to rethink and refine. Often, the Next Gen will have their own ideas about what constitutes good corporate governance, honed in business school classes and in discussions with the Next Gens of other family businesses. If the business is ultimately meant for the Next Gen, then it is a good idea to let them take a major part in improving the process and structure of the governance.

From wait your turn to horses for courses 07

Defy convention

CASE STUDY

Fictional case 7

Now almost 60, and chastened by his failure to make it big on his own, Fred has waited fifteen years for his turn at the top of the family business. Barely 30 and fresh from fruitful stints in engineering and environmental law, Jake wants to change the world and the company. Irascible but well-meaning, Fred thinks Jake is presumptuous. Impetuous but insouciant, Jake thinks Fred just doesn't get it. If you like, imagine a climactic meeting between the two second cousins, of the fourth and fifth generations, respectively. Fred wants to put Jake in his place. Jake will not accept anything less than a revolution. Inevitably, Fred flies into a rage and Jake reacts by storming out and closing the door on a career in the business. Except that's not how it happens.

Fred makes promises – a vital project here, a special mission there. Jake throws himself into the work. Several years pass without any major problems arising. There is always something to do, and small wins motivate Jake just enough to maintain a balance between ambition and satisfaction. A few more years, maybe a full decade of continuous career advancement, and Jake starts to turn into Fred. He still says he wants to change things. He still thinks of himself as a rebel. Fred knows better: Jake is well placed to continue the family legacy. When the time comes for Fred to hand over the reins, Jake will be ready. Except that real life isn't a straight line.

Young Jake won't wait; he knows better than to enter the golden cage. Instead of accepting the offer to join the business and work his way up, he tries to enlist the support of his own generation, siblings, first and second cousins, spread across several continents. Some of them say they care, others are indifferent but willing to listen. As an initial step, they form a chat group, 'Don't Tell Fred'. A subset of the most active chat participants eventually arranges to meet in a New York hotel. There is a lot they can agree on: the need for more transparency in the supply chain to improve labour conditions, the desirability of refreshing a stagnant product line, the drive for stronger shareholder rights. The fifth generation's ideas are bold, but not unrealistic. As they know from conversations with peers, other business families around the world are already doing similar things. The New York group hammers out a summary and shares it on the chat. To conclude the pow-wow, in person and virtual participants nominate a delegation of three to go talk to Fred. Now, the story starts.

The chosen three make a formal appointment to see Fred. They send him an agenda and prepare themselves for how they think he will react. When the big day dawns, the three cousins are ready. Meeting in the lobby of company headquarters thirty minutes before the appointed hour, they go through their notes one more time. United, they feel strong enough to parry whatever Fred will throw back at them. Older and more experienced, Jake is the leader and spokesperson, but the other two are right next to him, primed to pick up the ball, should Jake falter. At five to nine, they take the elevator up to Fred's office on the eleventh floor and check in with the secretary. They won't have to wait; at nine precisely, the double doors open and Fred welcomes them into his sanctuary. Leaving the mahogany desk off to one side, he asks them to join him on comfortable chairs arranged around a low coffee table. Family first, Fred kicks off the meeting by enquiring about their parents and their siblings. Next, he calls in the secretary to take orders for coffee and cookies. The three Next Gens are raring to get their points across, to fight it out if need be, but Fred seems to have all the time in the world. Too often, reality turns out to be an anticlimax.

After a full ten minutes of small talk that punctures the Next Gen's intensity balloon, Fred finally gets around to responding to their agenda and addressing their concerns. First off, he acknowledges the relevance of the suggestions made by the younger generation: the supply chain could benefit from an in-depth review; the age of the product line worries him as much as it worries them; and shareholder rights have been an issue of contention in the family for many years. He says that he would welcome their input. Why don't they put together a few concrete proposals for him to consider and take to the appropriate committees? Jake and his cousins were prepared for Fred to deflect or even flat-out reject their ideas, but they aren't quite ready to take the next step and work with him. He seems sincere about the need for change, he appears to welcome their input, but maybe he's putting up a front. There's no way to be sure. He's also given them a new challenge; concrete proposals require that they go back to the original group for approval and dedicate time to working out detailed solutions. The pressure is now on them to walk their talk.

Before they can muster more of a reaction than mute agreement, the meeting is over and Fred is ushering them out of his office – 'So sorry... an important phone call... counting on you, be sure to follow up.' Jake wants to go right back in to continue the meeting, as soon as Fred's phone call is over; the others are not convinced that now is the time to push their older cousin any further. They ought to first decide which issue means the most to them and their group. Do the others really care enough about the health of the product line or the state of shareholder rights to get involved in a full-scale review? A sustainable supply chain, energy efficient and with fair working conditions for everyone, both inside and outside the company, that's something they can probably all support – why not start there and get the wheels of change turning? In any case, it's going to take work, the company's supply chain is global and they have only a vague understanding of most of the intermediate steps. Fred did offer to help them by paying for consultants to do some of the work, but that would mean giving up control of the project, wouldn't it? It's all about momentum.

Reluctantly, Jake resolves to call it a day and go with the majority opinion. They arrange for an online meeting with the others and agree on how to take the project forward, assigning roles and setting deadlines. Someone remarks that Fred is testing their mettle. Of course he is, but they won't let him off easily this time. By keeping him in the loop of how their work is progressing, they'll make sure that he won't scuttle their efforts in the end. They engage a consultant, but not to do the work, only to provide structure and guidance. Jake is still the leader of the Next Gen, but the others also get their hands dirty. Two members of the group take it upon themselves to visit every node in the long chain, from the mouth, all the way back to the tree, meeting with retailers, shippers, traders, suppliers and sub-suppliers. They spend over three months gathering information, relying on their own eyes to see and their own ears to judge. Another member of the Next Gen consults with industry specialists to get a feel for the state of the art. As the evidence mounts, their initial doubts turn into suspicions and eventually into certainty: the family business – their family business – is not up to par. They have documented numerous instances of excessive fuel use and several cases of child labour. If the information they have were to leak out to the press, it would be enough to get the family in trouble. What started out as a research project aimed at motivating change from within has become deadly serious.

Fred acts surprised. He encourages the Next Gen to keep it under their hats, until he can figure out what to do about their findings. They want to call an extraordinary meeting of the family council. It won't be long until the whole world finds out.

The conceptual approach

Different views of time are often a primary source of conflict over roles in the family business, with a Current Gen attitude of 'Wait your turn' set against a Next Gen attitude of 'I won't wait'. Age has time and prefers continuity; youth never has time and feels compelled to act. To some extent, these attitudes merely represent a re-enactment of the classical parent letting go/child conquering adulthood dilemma, the older admonishing the younger to be patient and the younger impatient to venture forth and change the world – a replay of Cat Stevens' song *Father and Son*.

Understanding the generation gap in family business

In the context of the 21st century family business, the father (mother) and son (daughter) start even further apart and have more difficulty to relate than the model pair sung about by Cat Stevens. This is because of the marked contrast between what the Current Gen saw in their own youth and what the Next Gen are seeing now. The Current Gen of leaders will usually have had the experience of starting small, either as a founder who made something out of nothing or as an heir who worked his/her way up from an initial position of limited responsibility – youthfully impatient in their time, but constrained by opportunity and/or tradition. More often than not, business founders take great pride in having started out small and heirs who worked their way up look back upon their time in the depths of the family business as a formative experience. Before they could take on larger responsibilities, the Current Gen had to prove themselves, in the competitive marketplace and (or) in the family. Even if they started out from wealth, members of the Current Gen did not have the luxury of drawing on a full deck of business resources right away.

By contrast, and there is much more to it than just the impatience of youth, the Next Gen is characterized by big-picture thinking. As we have seen, firm-level questions of strategy, sustainability and governance concern the Next Gen just as much, if not more than learning on the job and personal career advancement. Not only that, they have grown up with evidence of very rapid change everywhere, with many of the most striking advances driven by young entrepreneurs and achieved over a short time span. Wherever one looks – technology, business, society or politics – the last twenty-five years have seen disruption on an unprecedented scale (see also Chapter 4). Great changes have happened very quickly and, in business at least, younger leaders like Jeff Bezos, Elon Musk or Mark Zuckerberg have often been in the driver's seat. Even where major transformations are concerned, speed has become the norm and youthful role models are showing the way. Family businesses see these developments playing out in the relationships between the Next Gen and the Current Gen. The Next Gen's inclination for big-picture thinking and rapid action can clash dramatically with the Current Gen's belief in waiting your turn.

What is better for the family business? The traditional response to youthful impatience is to divide and rule: give the Next Gen bite-sized problems to sharpen their teeth on and keep a watchful eye on their development in view of slowly building leaders for the future. It's the slow process of proving that one is ready, analogous to what the Current Gen once went through itself. Taking this logic one step further, some family businesses have organized project tournaments and investment contests in which members of the Next Gen compete against each other to show who is best suited to take over one day. In this manner, the doers can be separated from the dreamers and the business as a whole is not exposed to undue risk. But what if the Next Gen of today does not accept being shoehorned into specialist positions with little scope for making a real impact? What if they credibly threaten to take their talent and energy elsewhere, unless they can assume significant responsibility right away? Indeed, according to the most recent empirical research on the question, succession intentions among the Next Gen are low (less than 20 per cent) and declining.[1] With increased access to opportunities outside the family business, the most entrepreneurial may be the least likely to come back.[2] There has to be a better way than putting off the Next Gen's ambitions or trying to shelve their potential to contribute in meaningful ways – for the relationship between the generations and, just as importantly, for the business.

Building a more nuanced understanding of the different generations' roles

Building a more nuanced understanding of the respective roles of the Current Gen and the Next Gen in the family business represents a very important step in resolving the wait your turn/I'm ready now conflict. While the role of the Current Gen is well defined and commonly accepted – to lead the business and the family – the role of the Next Gen often remains vague and open to multiple interpretations. There may be a family constitution in place that defines rules for when and under what conditions family members can enter the family business; there may also be an established career plan for the Next Gen, but what do these documents have to say about what specific role(s) the individual members of the Next Gen are to play in the development of the business and the family? More often than not, the role of the individual is not defined early on and is left ambiguous, even as the family member progresses along a career trajectory. Is the Next Gen to focus on self-actualization or loyal service to the business and the family? On preparation for the long term or action for immediate results? On following orders or taking charge? On supporting continuity or driving change? The answers to these questions will be context specific and depend on the individuals involved and the business, but not facing up to the discussion or simply assuming set responses is not good enough in an age where youth-driven change has become a societal norm.

Discussion about the role(s) of the Next Gen can take place all along the early years of an individual's career, regardless of whether he/she is working outside or inside the confines of the family business. In fact, scheduling regular feedback sessions about an individual's career as it relates to their role in the family business can help keep the family member working outside close to the family business, while providing valuable perspective for the family member working inside. The goal is to ensure that every family member who wishes to do so finds the right place from which to contribute. In the ideal case, each member of the Next Gen will assume a role that fits his/her unique skills and propensities: thus, if an individual demonstrates the ability and the perseverance to make change happen, then his/her role in the family business can reflect that, regardless of age or seniority. On the other hand, if an individual shows a talent for optimizing existing processes – not all young people thrive on change – then the jobs he/she takes on can be tailored to administration and conservation. Even or maybe especially those members of the Next Gen who do not see a place for themselves in the day-to-day work of the family business can be kept abreast of developments and prepared for the responsibilities of ownership. It's about putting people in a position to succeed individually and feel at one with the family business. The size of the family talent pool is limited by the size of the family, and no family business today can assume that family members will necessarily make the effort to join and continue the work of the previous generations. Those who choose to do so represent the family's ongoing investment of human capital in the business. Just as for any other limited resource in business, it's good practice to try to make the most of it.

Generational transition, the Millennial Generation and mental age

A lot has been said about the Millennial Generation – it is reported to be particularly individualistic, but also collaborative in work settings and socially conscious.[3] Increased individualism as part of their make-up would seem to reduce the Next Gen's interest in devoting themselves to a career in the family business, while easier collaboration and, especially, higher social consciousness would argue for more interest in making the family business a good place to work.[4] Whichever way these effects play out, and this is likely to differ somewhat across cultures, no research has demonstrated that putative generational characteristics are of decisive importance in the relationship between the Current Gen and the Next Gen of family business leaders. Rather than delve any further into ambiguous comparisons of the youth of today with the youth of yesterday, therefore, we prefer to highlight the enduring generational characteristics that are linked to age. This approach seems the most salient, given our desire to understand not just the

Next Gen as it presents itself today, but the interplay of youth and maturity in the family business.

The last twenty years of research in psychology on the questions of age and mental age have been particularly productive and relevant. Cognitive ability is a function of age, but not in a straightforward way. Indeed, while getting older is associated with a loss of detailed memory and speed of thinking, it is also linked to an increase in the individual's ability to see a pattern in a mass of information.[5] Thus, while young adults are particularly adept at focusing their efforts and taking calculated risks, mature individuals (beyond 40) are better at recognizing the broad connections among issues (synthetic reasoning) and less likely to take risks, positive or negative.[6] In other words, and on average, their mental ages predispose the Current Gen and the Next Gen to process information differently and take different courses of action. This key finding has important implications for the respective roles of the generations in the family business. Individual exceptions notwithstanding, the Current Gen is cognitively hardwired to preserve what has been built, while the Next Gen is cognitively hardwired to push for change and engage in entrepreneurship. Taking research results from neuroscience and psychology into account helps explain some of the gaps observed between the Current Gen and the Next Gen, particularly in how they approach transformative change. Understanding the gap is the first step to bridging it. Rather than fighting natural proclivities, the Current Gen and the Next Gen can work to incorporate them into their planning and decision-making, for individual careers and for issues of importance to the family business as a whole.

Making negotiated choices about waiting your turn vs taking over now

As outlined above, where and how the Next Gen makes its entrepreneurial mark ought to be a matter of discussion between the generations, not a question of the Current Gen handing out assignments. What we are talking about here is making explicitly negotiated choices with respect to the role of the Next Gen. If the Next Gen is change-focused and committed, the Current Gen may defy convention about giving responsibility early and suppress their own fear of failure: let the Next Gen try their hand at major change. This can take all kinds of shapes, from the simple, like preparing research reports on questions of significance to the family business, all the way to the complex, like running transformation initiatives as described in the Introduction. (For more detail on how families can and do defy age conventions, including examples, see Chapter 10.) The point is that major change that goes to the heart of what the family business is about does not have to remain the exclusive province of the Current Gen of family business leaders. In many ways, the Next Gen may be better prepared and cognitively more apt to lead change than the Current Gen, ideally in close collaboration with and drawing upon the deep experience of the Current Gen.

Like legacy vs change, the juxtaposition discussed in Chapter 4, wait your turn vs take over now is a false dichotomy. Wait your turn vs take over now implies that leadership is absolute and can be entrusted to only one person or one generation at a time. Absolute leadership in turn puts a great deal of pressure on the singular event of succession – once every thirty years, or whenever the generation in power decides to step down or is pushed aside. With this kind of mindset there is very little room for genuine intergenerational collaboration on the issues that actually determine the future of the family business: strategy, sustainability and governance. Side by side represents a way to overcome this and other false dichotomies related to the traditional way of thinking about succession in family businesses. Rather than focusing on who is in power now and who will come to power in the future, side by side emphasizes the benefits to be had if the generations manage to work together today, from the shared decision on which issues to pursue to the joint implementation of solutions. Rather than highlighting and thus dramatizing the handover, side by side puts the accent on the process of finding agreement between the generations.

KEY TAKEAWAYS

1. The gap between experience and youth centres on the power to make change happen.
2. Experience and youth reflect different strengths, both of great value to the business.
3. Negotiated choice and joint action represent methods for bridging the generations.

Learning journey: Pit stop 7

Please refer to Chapter 12 for a full explanation of the educational approach supporting the learning journey.

SELF-LEARNING

Self-assessment

Assess where you and the other generation are and should be on the continuum between 'wait your turn' (patience) and 'horses for courses' (impatience).

Self-reflection (SR)

Current Gen: Think through the following statements. How true are they of your own situation?

The Next Gen is too impatient to take responsibility.

The Next Gen is at the heart of driving change.

The Next Gen's capabilities are put to best use.

Next Gen: Think through the following statements. How true are they of your own situation?

The Current Gen is too slow to share responsibility.

The Current Gen is in charge of the pace of change.

The Next Gen's capabilities are put to best use.

Development plan for Current Gen/Next Gen

Draw up a development plan in which you define the following milestones:

Short term: What will I do by next week to close the patience/impatience gap? What will I consider a success by then?

Medium term: What will I do by next month to close the patience/impatience gap? What will I consider a success by then?

Long term: What will I do by next year to close the patience/impatience gap? What will I consider a success by then?

Action review

Mark the dates in your calendar when you check how well you have achieved the short-, medium- and long-term goals you set. Evaluate what you have achieved and look back at what went well and what went poorly.

MODERATED WORKSHOP LEARNING

Group discussion

Use the material presented in Chapter 7 as a launch pad for thinking about and critically discussing how the family approaches the timing of sharing power.

For the Current Gen, first prepare yourself, then discuss with the Next Gen:

> What would it take, in your eyes, for the Next Gen to be ready to lead the family business?

For the Next Gen, first prepare yourself, then discuss with the Current Gen:

> If you were to take over the lead of the family business, what role would you foresee for the Current Gen?

Case discussion

Read fictional case 7 and discuss the following questions:

> *Put yourself in the position of Fred: why does Fred resist the involvement of Jake and the 5th generation?*
>
> *Put yourself in the position of Jake: why does Jake put so much effort into transforming the family business?*
>
> *As a consultant to the family, how would you advise Fred and Jake to collaborate to transform the family business?*

Case simulation

Replay the conversation between Fred and one of the cousins when the Next Gen presents the findings of their assessment in your own words.

For the Next Gen, assume the role of Fred.

For the Current Gen, assume the role of one of the cousins of the 5th generation.

Starting positions: Fred looks for ways to put off Jake and the 5th Gen; Jake and the 5th Gen confront Fred and the family.

Those who are not involved in the simulation observe and comment.

Development plan for Current Gen/Next Gen

Draw up a development plan in which you define the following milestones:

Short term: What will I do by next week to close the patience/impatience gap? What will I consider a success by then?

Medium term: What will I do by next month to close the patience/impatience gap? What will I consider a success by then?

Long term: What will I do by next year to close the patience/impatience gap? What will I consider a success by then?

Co-coaching

Choose a partner from a different generation and share your development plan with him or her. Arrange two follow-up meetings after two months and after six months to see how well you have implemented your plan.

CLASSROOM LEARNING

Group discussion

Use the material presented in Chapter 7 as a launch pad for thinking about and critically discussing how families approach the timing of sharing power.

What are the common hurdles in intergenerational transition processes?

What are key success factors in intergenerational transition processes?

Case discussion

Read fictional case 7 and discuss the following questions:

Put yourself in the position of Fred: why does Fred resist the involvement of Jake and the fifth generation?

Put yourself in the position of Jake: why does Jake put so much effort into transforming the family business?

As a consultant to the family, how would you advise Fred and Jake to collaborate to transform the family business?

Case simulation

Replay the conversation between Fred and one of the cousins when the Next Gen presents the findings of their assessment in your own words.

Starting positions: Fred looks for ways to put off Jake and the fifth generation; Jake and the fifth generation confront Fred and the family.

Those who are not involved in the simulation observe and comment.

Oxford-style debate

Form two teams and prepare to debate the following thesis, with one team in favour and the other team against:

> If the timing of the transition is determined solely by the Current Gen, it is often too late.

Conduct a debate to collect all possible and valid arguments for and against the proposal.

Case report

Choose a family business that you know or are familiar with and analyse how they managed the intergenerational transition process. Make concrete suggestions on how this process could be improved.

From dominant leadership to governance 08

Strengthen systems

CASE STUDY

Fictional case 8

'It's airtight, Herr Schmidt – the best shareholders' agreement we've ever written.'

'I'm not sure. What if laws change? What if tax treaties don't hold?'

This was the umpteenth time that Schmidt had asked Jaysons, a renowned London private client law firm, to re-examine the structuring of his succession. With every new iteration, he seemed to become more anxious. A man who had once turned his father's modest Tyrolean masonry business into a regional construction powerhouse by aggressively pushing out and buying up the competition, in old age Schmidt obsessed about maintaining control over his wealth and his family. His attitude towards risk had shifted with the sale of his company fifteen years ago. Lucky enough to catch the peak of the cycle and get rid of his construction companies for cash and at a very good price, Schmidt had emerged from the 2008 global financial crisis with a fortune in ready money. The divestment of his businesses had made him one of the richest men in the German-speaking world. No longer was Schmidt defined by the buildings he built; in public perception and in his own eyes, Schmidt was redefined by his wealth.

In construction, money was a means to an end, and Schmidt knew exactly how to use it. Money for the sake of money, on the other hand, brought with it a multitude of concerns that he did not have prior experience of. So many new people appeared out of nowhere to offer their so-called services. So many devices and dodges presented themselves for his consideration. So many eventualities needed to be accounted for, so many things could go wrong. Uncomfortable with the whole process, but keenly aware of the danger of abdicating at this point, Schmidt led from the front. He educated himself on the detail of wealth management, he consulted with independent experts and he spent many months thinking about how best to work with the money. Foremost on his mind was the desire to use the fortune to ensure the future of his family, not just that of his own children and grandchildren, but the future of many generations of Schmidts to come.

Schmidt wanted a single trusted interlocutor. Not for him the common practice of splitting his wealth among several service providers. No Vienna-based wealth management firm was big enough and sophisticated enough to satisfy his needs. In any case, his tax situation forced him to relocate to a more favourable country and plan across multiple jurisdictions. Eventually, after an exhaustive beauty contest involving the largest global accounting firms, the oldest Swiss private banks and the most reputable London lawyers, he chose Jaysons to structure and oversee all of his financial affairs. The accounting firms and the private banks could not hide the gaps left by departmental silos; the competing law firms could not muster the required reach. Jaysons had an answer for whatever Schmidt asked for, delivered seamlessly and catered to his situation.

The future scared him. He did not fear for himself, but for the wealth he had built up and for his family. He couldn't trust his daughters and sons – spendthrift egotists and ineffective judges of human character, in his eyes. Left to their own devices, they would lose it all in a very short time. He had to protect their future and he focused all of his energies on pursuing that objective. Every point, even the seemingly most peripheral detail, had to be considered and reconsidered: the legal domicile of the various holding companies, the shareholding structures of the businesses he had invested in, the allocation of beneficial ownership, the distribution of physical and financial assets and, above all, the question of his taxes. There should be no wiggle room for his heirs and no scope for error.

For Schmidt's four children, the price of participating in the bounty of inheritance was strict adherence to his rules. As long as they bowed to his strictures, and these included tight limitations on what professional activities they could pursue and how they could spend their money, they remained in his good graces and benefitted from his generosity. Once, his lone daughter had tried to strike out on her own, putting part of the money he had let her co-sign for into a California-based venture capital fund. Aware of the leak from early on, Schmidt let fatherly feelings get in the way of reason and did not intervene until her ill-advised adventure had created a sizeable tax liability for the family. Even then, he was gentle in reining her in, closing the investment behind her back and avoiding direct confrontation. Schmidt was determined not to let something like that happen a second time. Ever since that foiled escape attempt, he had focused more keenly on surveillance and control. If any one of them so much as thought about breaking from the fold, Schmidt would know about it and be able to take appropriate action immediately.

Still, Schmidt was restless. Even if the family was largely under control, many other uncertainties still had the potential to bring down the edifice that he had so carefully constructed. Every day, he thought of a new horror scenario. What if his eldest son died before he did? What if his second son ran the business he was in charge of into the ground? The solution set up by Jaysons was to segregate the various assets, protecting each investment separately, so that the loss of one would not affect any of the others. This so-called 'ring-fencing' appealed to Schmidt's sense of order and occupied his agitated mind. There was so much to ring-fence: his many holdings and their constituent companies, his convoluted financial assets across multiple jurisdictions, his children's properties and their marriages and, last but not least, the offshore trusts of his children's children.

A veritable maze of contracts and agreements had grown up around Schmidt and his family – so complex that Jaysons assigned one senior associate lawyer full-time just to keep track of it all. Although Jaysons were specialized in serving fabulously wealthy families, Schmidt was a case apart.

His lawyer was permanently on call, and Schmidt did not hesitate to contact him on his private number, day and night, even on holidays. With well-remunerated patience, the lawyer explained, soothed and took down new requests. Schmidt was relentless. On the surface, every new demand made sense, although some of the fresh clauses contradicted positions taken earlier and others opened up further issues. And yet, the lawyer was not naïve: he knew that Jaysons had become overly reliant on the outsized fees generated from the Schmidt account; he also knew that Schmidt's children chafed under the restrictions their father had imposed. More by luck than by design, he found himself in a position where a great many people depended on him.

Another Sunday evening, another call from Schmidt.

'Good evening, Mr Schmidt.'

'I want you to review the domicile of our Irish commodities investment vehicle. I am concerned about the political situation there and want to know how we can hedge against Sinn Féin gaining additional power and moving to undermine the regulatory conditions for tax optimization.'

'Yes, of course, but it will take time to research alternative locations.'

'No matter. Just do it.'

'I will get started immediately.'

'Another thing…'

'Yes, Mr Schmidt?' – 'Mr Schmidt?' – 'I say, Mr Schmidt?'

There was no response. – Regardless, the lawyer would get to work on the new request that very same evening.

But before doing that, he put in a call to Friedrich, Schmidt's youngest. Ireland was Friedrich's set-up; if something were to be changed in the Irish arrangements, Friedrich stood to lose the independence he had carved out for himself behind his father's back. Even worse, Schmidt might find out.

The conceptual approach

Founder-led businesses revolve around the founder – his/her personality, his/her leadership and his/her preferences for strategy and structure. The founder and the founding model, in turn, generally have a lasting impact on the organizational culture, that is to say the values of the company and the assumptions on which the values are based.[1] This description of the founder imprint on organizational culture holds not only for how the company runs its operations and treats its various stakeholders, but also for the leadership culture. Thus, the experience of an autocratic, omnipresent founder will encourage autocratic leadership behaviour in subsequent generations, while the experience of a hands-off leadership style in the founding years will lead to more laissez-faire leadership down the line. These founding effects tend to be more enduring in companies that remain family-run over generations, in contrast to the situation at companies that come under the control of non-family management.

Understanding dominant personal leadership

We observe that many multigenerational family businesses are still characterized by dominant personal leadership years after the founder has departed, with a son of the founder or a daughter of the founder's brother holding sway like the founder did and representing the face of the business. A dominant leader does not share power with others and is not constrained by institutional checks and balances; he/she runs the business as if it were a personal fiefdom. The imprint of an autocratic, dominant founder is only partially responsible for this state of affairs. After all, many family businesses do not start out with a dominant leader. Why then do we still see a preponderance of this kind of autocratic leadership behaviour in family businesses? It has to do with inattention to corporate governance. Unlike publicly listed firms, family businesses are not under the legal obligation to comply with any corporate governance codes. Although shareholdings may be increasingly dispersed as the generations succeed each other, many families' failure to take governance seriously favours a concentration of power in the hands of a single individual or, alternatively, a very small group or individuals.[2] When corporate governance has not been professionally addressed and formal institutions of family business governance like an ownership committee, a board of directors, or a family council, are absent or existing but ineffective, it is common to see the family business run by whoever manages to get the upper hand in the family.

One of the distinguishing positive characteristics of the family business in comparison to the firm with many unrelated shareholders is the long-term involvement of the family. The name of the people who represent the firm is the same as the name on the door. However, the commitment of the family does not necessarily imply dominant personal leadership and a concentration of power in one person or a few people. Indeed, some of the most long-lived and successful family businesses maintain a strong connection to the family without subjugating the firm to the dominance of particular individuals. As one would expect, examples include many of the family-dominated firms that are also publicly listed, i.e. Roche in Switzerland, Ford Motor Company in the United States or Møller-Maersk in Denmark; however, many firms still under 100 per cent private ownership – Hilti in Liechtenstein, Cargill in the United States, or Merck in Germany, to name just three of the most well known – have also emancipated themselves from dominant personal leadership. In these family businesses and many other smaller ones that have also moved away from dominant personal leadership, mutually agreed upon governance mechanisms such as ownership committees and boards of directors explicitly limit the power of individuals, and institutional relationships follow a set of rules that have been mutually agreed upon. Checks and balances of this kind have to be strong, but adaptable. In order to make sure that the rules stay relevant over generations, the governance agreements in these companies are not hewn in stone, established once and for all, but are open to revision if proper procedures are followed (see below for more on how existing governance arrangements can be adapted for every new generation).

For those family businesses characterized by a dominant leader, the arrival of a Next Gen that wants to make its mark poses an especially difficult challenge. The dominant leader whose power is based on his/her personal authority is far more likely to feel threatened by the Next Gen than the leader who is embedded in a widely accepted governance framework. In cases such as these, the Next Gen's effort to transition from hierarchical to peer-based relations with the Current Gen serves to throw a lack of effective governance in the family business into sharp relief. The default outcome of this process is the kind of conflictual rivalry described in Chapter 3, pitting one generation against the other and exacerbating conflicts within the generations. Eventually, the dominant leader in place beats back the young internal competition, or a new dominant leader emerges. It is a vicious cycle, potentially very harmful to the family business and certainly not conducive to collaboration between the generations.

Starting discussions about governance

How to overcome the vicious cycle of dominant leadership leading to more dominant leadership? In many cases that we have witnessed, members of the Next Gen are the originators of discussions about governance in family businesses characterized by dominant personal leadership. Knowledgeable about governance by virtue of their education and their interaction with other family businesses around the world, they see the dangers dominant personal leadership can pose to the viability of the firm.[3] A member of the Next Gen might be inspired to write a paper about governance in the family business for a class at university or in business school; he/she might then engage in discussions with professors and fellow students about how best to broach the subject back home; with or without the support of his/her siblings and/or cousins, finally, he/she will find the right time to discuss the paper with the Current Gen of leadership. In a sense, a discussion about governance then becomes the launch pad and the testing ground for changing the basis of relations between the generations.

On the surface, even the most authoritarian of Current Gen leaders may demonstrate openness to conducting a governance discussion or, in some cases, even a formal governance review under the guidance of a professional consultant (see Chapter 11 for more on the use of family business consultants). After all, everyone in some way connected to a family business is aware, at least at a theoretical level, of the danger of failure and the importance of governance to building a sustainable future for the family: a version of 'riches to rags in three generations' or 'shirtsleeves to shirtsleeves' exists in a great many languages. What's more, as long as the discussion stays at a general level and does not lead to questioning share ownership, board of director composition or leadership succession, progress is often smoother than expected, despite the potential impact of discussing issues that can upset the existing family equilibrium. Given the weight of the evidence from family business practice, it is hard to disagree with the need for functioning governance systems. In the abstract, a working ownership committee, an effective board of directors and an inclusive family council make sense to everybody. Indeed, many families get to the point of signing formal governance agreements before stepping back at the brink when one or another individual, or even a group of allied individuals, afraid of losing power for themselves or their branch, scuttles the process.

Agreeing upon governance changes and making them stick

Each family will have a different governance trajectory, but, for both the Current and the Next Gen, it is important to persevere in these discussions (see Chapter 11 on how to maintain momentum in change initiatives involving both generations, for governance, as well as for strategy and sustainability), to keep all key players involved (see Chapter 3 on fair process), but also to display determination. It may take several attempts and a number of years to put a working governance framework in place. The family business landscape is littered with governance projects that never came to fruition. There are three main reasons for the lack of follow-through:

1 Families tend to underestimate the *time* necessary to work through all the issues that need to be examined in order to agree upon and set up effective governance systems; busy Current Gen leaders, in particular, tend to quickly get impatient and lose interest in a project that does not have clear bottom-line implications.

2 Related to the question of time is the degree of *involvement*: delegation and committee work are fine as long as they don't compromise commitment; an easy yes to a white paper not discussed and not read in detail can never be taken for a definite yes.

3 Finally, fear of putting things in writing and giving family affairs a definite legal shape may also contribute to some family members pulling back from the brink at the moment of signing governance agreements.[4]

Many families try to do too much too soon. Particularly in family businesses built around a tradition of strong leaders and little formal governance, it can be advisable to proceed in small steps. Good governance and the sharing of power that goes with it need to be learned. Thus, it may be useful to start with something that everyone can agree upon relatively easily, like a family council, for example, to show that governance can, in fact, work and add value to the family and the business. In this process of putting governance in place, the Next Gen may play a key role, going beyond discussion and debate to demonstrate that they can make a real impact. The very policy of small steps may allow the Current Gen of leaders to see the benefit of working on governance with the Next Gen and, in so doing, strengthening the long-term robustness of the family business.

Reviewing and revising existing governance arrangements

In any case, all governance arrangements, even the most detailed, are subject to revision. Indeed, the possibility of revision, if there are the (shareholder) votes to do so, is a key ingredient in every governance agreement. Just as strategy changes to adapt to new market conditions, so should governance have the flexibility to change: in response to new strategic challenges *and* in response to new ownership setups.[5] Thus, expansion of the business into new markets may require changes in the board of directors, making it desirable to bring in people with relevant expertise. Family businesses that have not allowed for non-family board members in the past may need to consider adding independent directors. If there is a rule on the books prohibiting independent directors, this stricture would have to be reviewed, in line with governance arrangements that provide for amendment. Correspondingly, the ownership agreement can be written in such a way as to stipulate the possibility of change, should share ownership need to be re-examined, say to permit existing shareholders to sell some of their shares or to allow for a new, external shareholder. The process involved in reaching agreement and the formal document (articles of governance) provide a basis for governance and continuity in the family business, but no document, in all its clauses, can remain relevant forever.

Even where effective governance is in place, generational transition is often the occasion for reviewing processes and structures. What worked for one generation of family owners may not work for the next. In particular, governance bodies (i.e. ownership committee, board of directors and family council) and financial policies, as well as decision-making processes, require regular updating, if not complete revision, to suit the evolving needs of the family business and its owners. In other words, governance is never 'done'. Where should the initiative come from for reviewing family business governance, and how often should such an exercise be undertaken? In theory, any family member can initiate a governance review, as can non-family board members, if governance is part of their mandate. In practice, governance agreements can be structured in such a way as to provide not only mechanisms for amendment but also procedures for review, detailing under what circumstances a governance review can be triggered and what are the appropriate decision-making bodies to work with. As for timing, a good rule of thumb for family members and non-family members charged with responsibility for governance is never to assume that existing governance agreements still enjoy full support from all stakeholders in the family. This does not mean that governance is constantly up for grabs, to be turned inside out every year or even every three years. However, and in line with the emphasis on procedural fairness highlighted in Chapter 3, it is important that decision-makers keep their eyes and ears open to changes in the business and in the family that might require initiating a governance review.

KEY TAKEAWAYS

1. Dominant leaders and limited formal governance characterize many family businesses.
2. Members of the Next Gen are often the originators of discussions about improving governance.
3. Generational transition is a good occasion for reviewing structures and processes.

Learning journey: Pit stop 8

Please refer to Chapter 12 for a full explanation of the educational approach supporting the learning journey.

SELF-LEARNING

Self-assessment

Assess where you and the other generation are and should be on the continuum between dominant leadership and governance.

Self-reflection

Current Gen: Think through the following statements. How true are they of your own situation?

The governance of our family business works well – precisely as it should.

The Next Gen can and does play an important governance role.

We have the processes in place to keep governance current/relevant.

Next Gen: Think through the following statements. How true are they of your own situation?

The governance of our family business could be significantly improved.

The Next Gen can and does play an important governance role.

We have the processes in place to keep governance current/relevant.

Development plan for Current Gen/Next Gen

Draw up a development plan in which you define the following milestones:

Short term: What will I do by next week to close the dominance/governance gap? What will I consider a success by then?

Medium term: What will I do by next month to close the dominance/governance gap? What will I consider a success by then?

Long term: What will I do by next year to close the dominance/governance gap? What will I consider a success by then?

Action review

Mark the dates in your calendar when you check how well you have achieved the short-, medium- and long-term goals you set. Evaluate what you have achieved and look back at what went well and what went poorly.

MODERATED WORKSHOP LEARNING

Group discussion

Use the material presented in Chapter 8 as a launch pad for thinking about and critically discussing how the family approaches governance and power.

For the Current Gen, first prepare yourself, then discuss with the Next Gen:

> How would you describe the governance of the family business, what works well already, what needs more work?

For the Next Gen, first prepare yourself, then discuss with the Current Gen:

> How would you describe the governance of the family business, what works well already, what needs more work?

Case discussion

Read fictional case 8 and discuss the following questions:

> *Put yourself in the position of Schmidt: why does Schmidt go to such great lengths to keep control?*
>
> *Put yourself in the position of Schmidt's children: why don't Schmidt's children openly rebel against his controls?*
>
> *As a consultant to the family, (how) would you advise Schmidt and his children to reorganize their governance?*

Case simulation

Replay the conversation between the children and their father in your own words.

For the Next Gen, assume the role of the father, Mr Schmidt.

For the Current Gen, assume the role of the son, Friedrich.

Starting positions: Schmidt announces new controls on business decision-making; Schmidt's children discuss what to do.

Those who are not involved in the simulation observe and comment.

Development plan for Current Gen/Next Gen

Draw up a development plan in which you define the following milestones:

Short term: What will I do by next week to close the dominance/governance gap? What will I consider a success by then?

Medium term: What will I do by next month to close the dominance/governance gap? What will I consider a success by then?

Long term: What will I do by next year to close the dominance/governance gap? What will I consider a success by then?

Co-coaching

Choose a partner from a different generation and share your development plan with him or her. Arrange two follow-up meetings after two months and after six months to see how well you have implemented your plan.

CLASSROOM LEARNING

Group discussion

Use the material presented in Chapter 8 as a launch pad for thinking about and critically discussing how families approach governance and power.

What are the obstacles that prevent founder-led family firms from adopting transparent and effective governance structures?

What circumstances can facilitate the transition from founder-centric leadership to effective governance structures?

Case discussion

Read fictional case 8 and discuss the following questions:

Put yourself in the position of Schmidt: why does Schmidt go to such great lengths to keep control?

Put yourself in the position of Schmidt's children: why don't Schmidt's children openly rebel against his controls?

As a consultant to the family, (how) would you advise Schmidt and his children to reorganize their governance?

Case simulation

Replay the conversation between the children and their father in your own words.

Starting positions: Schmidt announces new controls on business decision-making; Schmidt's children discuss what to do.

Those who are not involved in the simulation observe and comment.

Oxford-style debate

Form two teams and prepare to debate the following thesis, with one team in favour and the other team against:

> Dominant leaders never leave voluntarily. They need to be pushed out, even in a family business.

Conduct a debate to collect all possible and valid arguments for and against the proposal.

Case report

Choose a family business that you know or are familiar with and analyse how they successfully transitioned from founder-led leadership to an effective governance process. Make concrete suggestions on how this transition can be further developed.

From succession to co-evolution 09

Grow leaders

CASE STUDY

Fictional case 9

It's not as if I'm just waking up to this massive deal. Ever since we had the first conversations with the investment bankers and with the lawyers, I've been closely involved. Not on every phone call and every meeting, mind you, but on all the important ones. This Holzmann acquisition is the kids' brainchild, but each time I could have called for a halt or at least for a slowdown in the proceedings, I gave the green light. Maybe I got carried away with the challenge; maybe I wanted to see how far they could run with it. Anyway, it's all gone very quickly, probably too quickly. What are three months, when you're talking about sixty years of company history and three billion dollars?

The truth is, the size of this thing blows me away. In one fell swoop, we are taking on a huge amount of debt, making Germany our number one market and grabbing the role of transmission parts supplier to Porsche and the entire Volkswagen group. If we get this right, it will be worth ten years of growth. Talk about 'Go big or go home!' Terribly exciting or very scary – it all depends on how you look at it. I don't know quite what to think.

Not that I don't want it to go through. It's the next logical step in our long-term plan, I get it. If we want to strengthen our position and hold off the competition, we don't have a choice but to make a decisive move at some point. I'm really proud of what the kids have put together here: how they established the contacts, negotiated the terms and put us in pole position to win the deal. A few years ago, when I was still running the show, I could never have imagined us getting this far. This is the kind of once-in-a-decade opportunity we've been preparing for. To think how far we've come since my grandfather opened up his shop back in 1953. Hard to believe that what started as a corner garage in Muncie, Indiana is now on the verge of becoming a global player.

Dad was the one who made this business, who set the stage for everything that was to come. It was his idea to sell the garages and start manufacturing. Unfortunately, Dad also held on for too long, kept us all under his thumb until the very last day. My sister was in accounts until the day she left the job to get married; I stayed in production, overseeing manufacturing until the day Dad died and I was forced to take over the whole thing. After fifteen years of running our plants, you can't say I wasn't prepared to take on more, but I wasn't ready to step into his shoes. I still had a lot to learn. Dad was a great business man, a good salesman and a brilliant negotiator, but he wasn't interested in planning for the future of the company and he certainly didn't want to share power with me or with anyone else.

I was never going to make the same mistakes he made. In the first year after Dad passed, I set up a board of directors to help me take the business to the next level of professionalism. I also started hiring from outside the local area and promoting the best people to positions of real importance. Most importantly, I paved the way for the kids to take over. Jack's been involved in every major decision since his twentieth birthday and Suzanne has always had her nose in the business.

Jack turned 35 last month and Suzanne's 32. They're old enough to run the show. Just look at how our growth has exploded in the five years since they formally joined me in the front office: there's no way I could have shouldered that on my own. It's all down to their drive. The more I ask of them, the higher they set the bar. Jack's proven himself in battle after battle, and Suzanne knows the numbers better than anybody. He's got the shirtsleeves and the guts, he's the doer; she's got the eyes to see and the nose to smell what really counts, she's the strategist.

Of course, they don't always agree, they discuss, they argue, but it never gets personal. Other families should be so lucky. Together, they're a Dream Team. It's their company, has been that way for a while already, if I'm honest with myself. They know it, too. Holzmann is their deal: they found it, they pushed for it and now they're ready to bring it home.

Time for me to do my own thing, they don't really need me here anymore. As the saying goes, 'Entrepreneurs never get old, they only run out of time.' Fifty-seven's not over the hill… I've got my best years ahead of me, right? For the first time in my life I'll have a clean slate. Who says I can't make it big by myself? My experience in high-end machine tooling and my inside knowledge of the automobile industry could make for some real breakthroughs, I reckon. It would be great fun to pitch some of my crazier ideas. Start-up scene, black sweater and jeans, here I come. Yeah, right!

I just don't know whom I can talk to about the Holzmann story, whom I can share my worries with. It has to stay top secret, so the circle of people I can consult is really small. My wife believes in the kids first and foremost; she won't have an ear for my doubts. My sister is too far away from the business these days to be of any real help. The board members have already given their OK on the deal. They asked all the questions that needed to be asked and were satisfied with the answers they got from Suzanne and the reassurances Jack gave them about being able to handle it; they won't want to go back on their word.

Everything's changing so fast. Make or break, that's what the Holzmann deal looks like to me. So much fresh debt on the books! Dad never wanted to borrow a penny. Such a big fish to swallow and in Germany, no less. It could take years for us to integrate the two companies. Smarter people than us have killed good businesses by taking on more than they can handle. Getting too big for our britches, that's what people around Muncie would say, if they knew what we were planning. The day the deal is announced, they'll be sure to say it.

Alone, I could never handle that kind of risk. Safety first has always been my mantra in the factory, in the business, in the family. It's just not in me to bet the house on one hand of cards. I know the numbers check out. It all looks good on paper. Don't get me wrong, I'm proud of my kids and the work they have done to put this together, but, boy, am I scared.

It's not too late; I could hold up the deal. They'll need my final approval – after all, I still hold the majority. When we looked at it a few years ago, the tax people thought it would be a good idea if I completely revamped the ownership structure and made Jack and Suzanne the biggest shareholders. How wise I was to say no and hold on to most of my shares.

One call from me and Holzmann is history, or at least put in a holding pattern, until I can get more comfortable with the whole thing. Of course, we're not the only ones on to Holzmann, it's not every day that one of the crown jewels of German precision manufacturing comes up for sale. We know of at least two other serious suitors. One call from me and we would probably lose the deal.

One call from me and we're back to square one. I don't know if Jack and Suzanne would ever forgive me if I ruined this thing. They've put so much time and energy into it, I can't pull the rug out from under their feet now, at the last minute. It would be going against everything I ever said about wanting to share the responsibility with them, about wanting them to make it their company.

Shades of Dad, I guess. Wonder what he would say. He would never have let them run this far without putting his foot down, that's for sure.

I don't know what to do… I really don't know.

The conceptual approach

By etymology and in modern business practice, the word 'succession' means taking another's place. In French, 'la succession' retains the original meaning of the word – the inheritance of someone who has passed on or moved on. Taking another's place is the antithesis of the co-evolution process described in this book. Succession entails a definite cut; side by side involves working together over years and sharing responsibilities. Succession at the top is often experienced as a dramatic event, a source of anguish for both the leaders involved and the organization. The sense of upheaval will be particularly strong in those family- and founder-led businesses characterized by dominant personal leadership. The passing of the baton comes to be seen as the end of an era. When it works as intended, succession planning is supposed to reduce the drama and alleviate the disruption. Well executed, succession planning paves the way for a smooth transition. In fact, many family businesses do not have concrete succession plans. Figures vary by country and by definition of what constitutes a succession plan, but most studies report that over half of family businesses do not have formally documented succession plans.[1] In other words, and although they depend to a much higher degree on key persons as leaders (as described in Chapter 8), the average family business lags far behind listed companies in the attention it affords to the issue of leadership succession.

Succession plans for the family business

In listed companies, formal succession plans for the C-suite and the board of directors are a required part of doing business: regulators impose and/or shareholders expect detailed contingency plans. In family businesses, on the other hand, stakeholder requirements with regard to succession are typically not spelled out. The family business does not *have to have* a succession plan in place. Formal requirements aside, practical obstacles and psychological fears often stand in the way of family business decision-makers engaging in succession planning. Many family business leaders are too busy with the business of doing business to devote the time necessary to do justice to succession planning. They can't or won't make the time needed to meet with lawyers and tax advisers specialized in addressing the ins-and-outs of preparing and executing a fully fledged succession. Unwillingness to spend time thinking about succession is not only a function of being too busy. As numerous psychologists have pointed out, facing a fully fledged succession also implies facing mortality and many leaders prefer to put off the day as long as possible.[2] Will the business outlive its leadership? What's left after a career in the business? Does handing over the reins hasten personal decline? In view of the effort and the anguish customarily associated with succession, it is understandable that many family business leaders try to avoid succession planning altogether.

Even with professional succession planning in place, handing over ultimate power is no easy matter and success in terms of perpetuating the family business is not guaranteed. The trouble in many cases is that succession planning occurs only periodically, at long intervals, and is not integrated into the regular governance of the family business. As currently conceived, succession planning invariably revolves around a rare event – the retirement of the Current Gen and the takeover of the Next Gen. Carried out in this way – as a once-in-a-lifetime occurrence, highly significant for the individuals concerned and essential to the survival of the family business – succession carries all the connotations of classical drama. No wonder modern television audiences cannot get enough of the fictional version. Side by side takes (some of) the drama out of succession. Instead of being defined as a critical episode in the life of the business, to be suffered through once every thirty years, or whenever the Current Gen leader becomes too frail to hold on to power, our approach recasts leadership transition as a continuous process. Working together over many years on key issues, the Current and the Next Gens shape succession together: rather than taking the form of an unusual occurrence, succession becomes part of the fabric of the family business. Rivalry, entrenchment and, indeed, disappointment over the ultimate choices made do not disappear with side by side. However, and as we will see in Chapter 10, implementing side by side between the generations reduces the probability that succession ends in conflict and crisis.

Succession as process

Scholarly research in the area of planning for senior leadership transition supports the 'succession as process' point of view, with an emphasis on procedural rationality and thorough information processing by the group of people responsible for choosing a successor.[3] In other words, succession at senior levels takes a considerable amount of time, involving extensive preparation and deliberation, leading to well-informed choices. In the family business, the succession process is often less formal than in the listed firm, but it can be seen as lasting much longer. In effect, the entire process of bringing the Next Gen up to speed, from initiation into the firm all the way to formal accession to leadership, may be understood as a succession process in which 'familiness', or the unique bundle of resources and capabilities that characterizes the family firm, is gradually transferred from one generation to the next.[4] Taking this idea one step further, some scholars have suggested that an extended transition can be viewed as a period of co-governance between the generations.[5] Our observations of the generations working side by side confirms these characterizations – the transfer of familiness and a period of co-governance – and takes the argument one step further. From our point of view, the very notion of succession as a discrete moment in time when power changes hands ought to be re-thought. Seen as a vital governance process, succession in the family business takes place over an extended period of time and focuses on collaboration between the generations, a gradual sharing of power rather than a distinct transfer of power.[6]

We do not wish to imply that the Next Gen is ready to share power right away, straight out of college or fresh from a first job. Accepted wisdom says that the Next Gen has to work its way up. This is a valid concern, not least to counter suspicions of nepotism and prove to non-family employees of the business that the Next Gen is deserving. At the same time, it is important to acknowledge that the Next Gen is different from the average employee in that they are being prepared to assume a leadership position, of the executive, of the board, of the ownership committee, or of the family council. The Next Gen characteristically feel an acute sense of commitment towards the future of the business and the family. As we have seen, they want to make an impact, sooner rather than later. Preparation for leadership and commitment to leadership come together in the kind of strategy, sustainability and governance transformation initiatives we have described in the introduction.

It is in the course of working side by side with the Current Gen on initiatives such as these that the Next Gen of today learns the ropes of the family business *and* gradually assumes the mantle of leadership. In this way, succession becomes a by-product of productive collaboration between the generations.

New ways of thinking about succession

Recall the points of departure for this book: first, the observation that the Current Gen of family business leaders remains healthy and at the helm for far longer than their predecessors; and second, the recognition that today's Next Gen has extraordinary potential to make an immediate contribution to the family business. If the traditional model of succession were to be applied to this novel situation, the Next Gen would be well over 50 years old before they finally took the reins and the business would have missed out on twenty or more of their most productive years as leading contributors. Think about Prince Charles, who took over from his mother, Queen Elizabeth, at the ripe age of 73. In the family business of today, what Next Gen would be willing to wait for a lifetime? With the traditional succession model, the exit of the Next Gen and/or bitter conflict between the generations are likely scenarios. Succession, as conceived of for so long, not only in family business, but more generally, is an all-or-nothing proposition – the original binary system in computing terms. In a context characterized by the longevity of the Current Gen and precociousness of the Next Gen, there is a need to find a different way to transition between the generations, with new roles and new modes of collaboration. This is why so many business families are experimenting with new ways of thinking about and actually implementing succession.

As noted in Chapter 7, both the Current and the Next Gens have a specific role to play in the life of the family business, the current as a guarantor of stability, the next as a catalyst for the future. On the surface, stability and the flexibility required to ensure future readiness may seem incompatible, a recipe for conflict over who is in charge and what is the right strategic direction. How can the guarantor of stability and the catalyst for the future work side by side? Established principles of corporate governance would suggest that, at some point, there has to be a clean break, with one generation of leaders taking over from the other. From a narrow perspective on governance as constraint, ambiguity over who is in charge is dangerous; what is called for is a clear division of tasks and a definite assignment of powers. Unless a clean break takes place, so the argument goes, the Current Gen will continue to meddle in the affairs of the business and get in the way of change, even if they have nominally handed over the baton, and the Next Gen will be thwarted in its efforts to establish control. Good governance is all about separating powers.[7]

Stepping down or stepping back

In the reality of many family businesses, however, the Current Gen does not step down, at least not completely. Instead, it *steps back*. Thus, the Current Gen may give up its executive position but remain the majority shareholder or resign from the board but retain informal influence over the family and the business. Unlike in the case of publicly listed companies, clean breaks are the exception in family businesses. Through share ownership and/or by means of personal reputation, the Current Gen often continues to have a role to play, even after the formal process of succession has been completed and the Next Gen has assumed the positions of leadership. Notwithstanding the principles of good corporate governance, this is not necessarily a bad thing. Stepping back from some of the formal trappings of power, i.e. from the CEO position to become chairperson of the board of directors, or from the chair to become senior adviser, the Current Gen can give the Next Gen space to reshape the family business, while still staying involved as an important resource. The first thing one thinks of is wise counsel. In other words, the older generation has the ability to take the long view and offer the younger generation the benefit of a different perspective based on leadership experience but tempered by detachment. Over and above counsel, the leaders who have stepped back from day-to-day involvement can play an important role in maintaining the backing of various stakeholders: shareholders from different branches of the family, important customers and senior staff who they themselves once hired and put in positions of responsibility. Most importantly, perhaps, the former leader(s) can provide moral support when big decisions need to be made, i.e. strategic shifts, major acquisitions or key executive hires. In the ideal case, the former leader(s) of the family business puts his/her own preferences aside and acts as a force behind the Next Gen's push for adaptation and renewal.[8]

Taking a formal step back in the manner described means little, of course, if the old parent/child hierarchy remains in place and the Current Gen continues to manage or even micromanage everything from backstage. These are the well-known dangers of not making a clean break and many family businesses suffer from incomplete succession. As we will show in Chapter 10, providing the Current Gen with real career alternatives, inside and outside of the family business, can reduce the likelihood of incomplete departures or unwanted comebacks. The point is that there has to be something after succession: the succession process is not complete until the generation that is moving on has found new goals to pursue. One way is for the Current Gen to engage in entirely new pursuits, unrelated to the family business. A realistic alternative is stepping back, i.e. handing off ultimate responsibility, but maintaining a supportive hand in the business. This can work well, if both generations have a clear understanding of their respective roles, if they have mature trust in each other's judgement and appreciate each other's capabilities.

A lot depends on the respective personalities – of the retiring leaders and of the emerging leaders. Some individuals are simply unable to take a back seat. If this is the case, a clear separation of powers remains desirable. On the other hand, and acknowledging personality differences, implementing succession as a process that starts when the generations are still young and continues even after power has formally been handed over has the potential to provide the best of two worlds: the Next Gen as the catalyst for the future in charge, the Current Gen as the guarantor for stability in support. If the generations have enjoyed a shared history of successfully working side by side, the vision outlined here has a good chance of becoming reality. In effect, working side by side from early on prepares the generations for the formal step of leadership succession, not as a singular break with the past, but as a steady process of transition.

KEY TAKEAWAYS

1. Despite relying on key people, many family businesses do not have succession plans.
2. When it involves multiple generations from early on, succession is a change process.
3. A quality succession process develops both generations, the Current and the Next.

Learning journey: Pit stop 9

Please refer to Chapter 12 for a full explanation of the educational approach supporting the learning journey.

SELF-LEARNING

Self-assessment

Assess where you and the other generation are and should be on the continuum between letting go and taking over.

Self-reflection

Current Gen: Think through the following statements. How true are they of your own situation?

Succession planning is a priority for us.

Every member of the family has found the right role.

The Current Gen and the Next Gen share a common succession vision.

Next Gen: Think through the following statements. How true are they of your own situation?

Succession planning is a priority for us.

Every member of the family has found the right role.

The Current Gen and the Next Gen share a common succession vision.

Development plan for Current Gen/Next Gen

Draw up a development plan in which you define the following milestones:

Short term: What will I do by next week to close the taking over/letting go gap? What will I consider a success by then?

Medium term: What will I do by next month to close the taking over/letting go gap? What will I consider a success by then?

Long term: What will I do by next year to close the taking over/letting go gap? What will I consider a success by then?

Action review

Mark the dates in your calendar when you check how well you have achieved the short-, medium- and long-term goals you set. Evaluate what you have achieved and look back at what went well and what went poorly.

MODERATED WORKSHOP LEARNING

Group discussion

Use the material presented in Chapter 9 as a launch pad for thinking about and critically discussing how the family approaches succession and succession planning.

For the Current Gen, first prepare yourself, then discuss with the Next Gen:

How would you describe the succession plans in your family business (what, how, who)?

What do you see as your future role?

For the Next Gen, first prepare yourself, then discuss with the Current Gen:

How would you describe the succession plans in your family business (what, how, who)?

What do you see as your future role?

Case discussion

Read fictional case 9 and discuss the following questions:

Put yourself in the position of the father: why does the father have so much difficulty letting go?

Put yourself in the position of Jack and Suzanne: have they done everything they could to reassure their father?

As a consultant to the family, how would you advise the father to deal with the Holzmann acquisition?

Case simulation

Replay the conversation between the children and their father in your own words.

For the Next Gen, assume the role of the father.

For the Current Gen, assume the role of Jack.

Starting positions: the father pulls the rug on the Holzmann acquisition at the last minute; Jack and Suzanne react.

Those who are not involved in the simulation observe and comment.

Development plan for Current Gen/Next Gen

Draw up a development plan in which you define the following milestones:

Short term: What will I do by next week to close the taking over/letting go gap? What will I consider a success by then?

Medium term: What will I do by next month to close the taking over/letting go gap? What will I consider a success by then?

Long term: What will I do by next year to close the taking over/letting go gap? What will I consider a success by then?

Co-coaching

Choose a partner from a different generation and share your development plan with him or her. Arrange two follow-up meetings after two months and after six months to see how well you have implemented your plan.

CLASSROOM LEARNING

Group discussion

Use the material presented in Chapter 9 as a launch pad for thinking about and critically discussing how families approach succession and succession planning.

What conditions facilitate a co-evolutionary intergenerational transition in a family business?

What conditions may impede a co-evolutionary intergenerational transition in a family business?

Case discussion

Read fictional case 9 and discuss the following questions:

Put yourself in the position of the father: why does the father have so much difficulty letting go?

Put yourself in the position of Jack and Suzanne: have they done everything they could to reassure their father?

As a consultant to the family, how would you advise the father to deal with the Holzmann acquisition?

Case simulation

Replay the conversation between the children and their father in your own words.

Starting positions: the father pulls the rug on the Holzmann acquisition at the last minute; Jack and Suzanne react.

Those who are not involved in the simulation observe and comment.

Oxford-style debate

Form two teams and prepare to debate the following thesis, with one team in favour and the other team against:

A co-evolutionary transition in the family business is only possible if both generations give up some of their power.

Conduct a debate to collect all possible and valid arguments for and against the proposal.

Case report

Choose a family business that you know or are familiar with and analyse how they managed the intergenerational transition and whether it was co-evolutionary in nature. Make concrete suggestions on how to further improve the process.

PART FOUR Navigating the transition

Action

> It's the action, not the fruit of the action, that's important. You have to do the right thing. It may not be in your power, may not be in your time, that there'll be any fruit. But that doesn't mean you stop doing the right thing. You may never know what results come from your action. But if you do nothing, there will be no result.
>
> MAHATMA GHANDI

> If you can't fly – then run. If you can't run – then walk. If you can't walk – then crawl. But whatever you do, you have to keep moving forward.
>
> MARTIN LUTHER KING JR

These two quotes may not seem immediately relevant to the family business context. After all, both Ghandi and King were concerned with the fate of entire peoples, not organizations. And yet, the difficulties they encountered – resistance, discouragement and the feeling of not being up to the task – have parallels in every context facing transition and change. From among the many thousands, even millions, of calls to action and quotes about action that human beings from the world over have recorded for posterity, we found these two to be particularly inspirational. Navigating the transition between generations in a family business is not existential for the world, but it is existential for the family business. In this sense, then, the words of Ghandi and King may ring true to the members of the Current Gen and the Next Gen looking for a new way to relate to each other in grappling with the challenges of succession. Navigating the transition is about leadership: doing the right thing and moving forward.

To offer a better understanding of what it takes to *support the shift* from hierarchical to peer-based relations between the generations, and from succession to co-evolution as a model for family businesses, we complement the analysis of trust maturity, capability appreciation and role respect presented in Parts One, Two and Three with descriptions of the *leadership practices* that families can put to use in the transition process. The recognition of generational transition as a journey implies the need to employ distinctive leadership practices that work over time, in different doses and in different ways, as the transition progresses. It is not a question of 'If stage X, then do Y'. Instead, families work with leadership practices that can be applied across stages and regulate how the generations interact. What we observe in the field is the pairing of a leadership practice that promotes the individual and aspirational with a leadership practice that upholds the collective and foundational, a dynamic tension between allowing individuals to maximize their potential and getting the basics right to ensure collective standards (Chapter 10). Since transformation initiatives can play a critical role in establishing peer-to-peer collaboration between the generations, we offer a practical guide on how to run them, with a variety of examples that cover the launch of a transformation initiative, maintaining momentum, embedding in the organization and conclusion (Chapter 11). Each family business faces its own particular context and works out its own path. Describing what can be done and what has been done, rather than what should be done, this book is intended as a resource for family businesses: to help readers find what they need, develop techniques for talking about it and share what works for them with a broader community. To support self-learning, moderated workshop learning and classroom learning for families and students of family businesses, we provide advice based on our teaching and consulting experience, and show how to use the different pedagogical tools recommended in this book (Chapter 12).

Learning approach: Side by side as action

Whereas the first three parts of the book make use of fictional case studies to initiate discussion, the fourth part draws on the lessons from original company histories to provide baselines to work with in implementing the side-by-side approach to generational transition in practice. The reason for this change in the type of material used as examples is didactic and pedagogical: whereas fictional case studies are particularly well suited to illustrating concepts and encouraging critical discussion, company histories are more appropriate for demonstrating different ways of implementing business changes. The original company histories we present draw from our involvement with a large variety of family businesses around the world, but remain anonymous. We want to stress that baseline examples are not recipes, and taking action in the family business is never a simple matter of adopting the experience of others, however successful. Every family is unique, and no general rules can be expected to apply across the board, without significant adaptation. Thus it is in the spirit of suggesting possible ways forward that we share the practical experiences of the business families we have worked with and studied.

- **Point of departure**
  → *Action means commitment from the Current Gen and the Next Gen.* The side-by-side mindset develops over time and builds on experience. Learning by doing is the watchword, with ample experimentation, extensive feedback and continuous improvement. Action is more important than talk of action, but open communication between the generations is critical for establishing clarity and obtaining buy-in. In this sense, trust maturity, capability appreciation and role respect are enablers. Wherever a family starts on the continuum of hierarchical to peer-based relations between the different generations, it is important that the movement goes in the right direction. Throughout the process of generational transition, therefore, transformation initiatives that require inputs from both generations and depend on generating agreement about the future of the family business can play a very important role in strengthening both the business and the family.

- **Important assumptions**
  → *Generational transition is a process; each family business works out its own path.* There is no silver bullet; while there may be some general principles that can guide action, the process itself yields specific learning

for each family, and it is important that families remain open to learning about themselves throughout the process. It is of course certainly not a bad idea for families and their advisers to familiarize themselves with the basic tenets of change management. Building recognition of the need for action, mapping out a transition plan and following up on the plan with action reviews that identify the challenges to be overcome are fundamental steps in any change process.[1] In the specific context of the family business, however, research indicates that willingness to spend enough time to fully involve the family and openness to make necessary adaptations along the way are the most important predictors of success.[2]

- **Normative implications**

  → *Develop a transition process that serves the business* and *engages the generations.* Business and family are equally important. Some family business leaders focus entirely on the day-to-day activity of the business and forget the family until it's too late to talk about succession. Others spend so much time and effort bringing the family along that the business suffers. In the family business, generational transition involves both the business *and* the family.[3] This means that recommendations for the business must consider the developmental state of the family (in terms of governance) and recommendations for the family must consider the economic state of the business (in terms of strategy and investment). Rather than looking for ready-made answers from the best practices of others, the challenge is for family members and their advisers to come up with and agree upon solutions that uniquely fit the business and the family.

Leadership practices 10

Promote the aspirational and uphold the foundational

In our research, we were struck by families' willingness to enter unchartered waters and try new approaches in supporting the process of generational transition. Thus, a US business family with significant interests in several sectors makes it a practice to include the Next Gen in all major strategic decisions from their early twenties onwards and has already set a departure date for the Current Gen CEO. Why do they place so much faith in the Next Gen? Further along in the transition process, a European machine technology business asks the family's heir apparent to take over and turn around an ailing foreign subsidiary, a Herculean task with poor odds of success. How do they dare to run the risk of letting their future leader fail? At the point of formal succession, finally, the founder of a Swiss medical business entrusts the family jewels to his son and, rather than continuing to oversee from the chair, moves on to a new venture. What kind of rationale underlies this remarkably clear-cut succession? These examples may appear radical, but, in our observations, they are not unusual. There is method to these and other families' unconventional actions.

We find that many families have come to view succession from one generation to the next as an extended transition process, rather than as a singular event (see also Chapter 9). The recognition of generational transition as a journey implies the need to employ distinctive leadership practices that work over time, in different doses and in different ways, as the transition progresses. It is not a question of 'If stage X, then do Y'; instead, families work with leadership practices that can be applied across stages and regulate how the generations interact. Intriguingly, we often observe the pairing of a leadership practice that promotes the individual and aspirational with a leadership practice that upholds the collective and foundational, that is to say a dynamic tension between allowing individuals to maximize their potential and getting the basics right to ensure collective standards. In actual experience, family businesses tend to move back and forth between the paired practices over time, adjusting for too great a degree of individual self-determination or too much collective discipline, as the situation demands.

In our work with business families, three pairs of leadership practices stand out and seem to work particularly well in facilitating generational transition and supporting trust maturity, capability appreciation and role respect:

Defy age preconceptions	AND	*Enforce behavioural norms*
Set outsized challenges	AND	*Install safety nets*
Empower freedom of choice	AND	*Assign responsibilities*

Over the following pages we want to describe how these paired leadership practices work, and provide the conceptual background underpinning their function in the family business context. The key notion to bear in mind in understanding and making use of this chapter is the dynamic tension between empowering the individual family member and maintaining the collective organization. As always, the caveat that each family has to find its own way applies.

Defy age preconceptions and enforce behavioural norms (supporting trust maturity)

Let us return to the US family business cited at the beginning of this chapter. On the one hand, family members defy age preconceptions by involving the Next Gen in major strategy decisions from the time they are in university; on the other hand, they enforce strong behavioural norms such as preparation for, attendance at and contribution (both form and content) to all-hands strategy meetings. You are included as a Next Gen, yes, but you had better not miss the meeting or arrive unprepared. In this example, the individual/aspirational leadership practice and the collective/foundational leadership practice are implemented simultaneously, balanced like yin and yang in Chinese philosophy. In other examples we have come across, defying age preconceptions comes first, to be reined in later by enforcing behavioural norms. Of critical importance, there is a degree of tension or pressure built into the duality between the two opposing but complementary leadership practices that keeps both generations on their toes.

It is not easy to defy age preconceptions. In fact, age preconceptions are fundamental to how human beings make sense of each other, on a par with race and gender in marking first impressions, and the topic has a prominent place in social psychology.[1] In the context of the family business, age preconceptions suggest that older family members (i.e. the Current Gen) are expected to do 'old' things, like administer, control and hang on, while younger family members (i.e. the Next Gen) are expected to take on small tasks, try their hands at many things and grow slowly into more significant responsibility. Defying age preconceptions, on the other hand, implies the Current Gen and the Next Gen understanding each other beyond stereotypes. Indeed, defying age preconceptions also contradicts some of the scientifically validated generalizations discussed earlier in this book, such as legacy vs change (Chapter 4) and old brain vs young brain (Chapter 7). In other words, family businesses that are actively defying age preconceptions are really going against the grain.

Why would they do so? In some cases, there may be historical precedent, as the family might have a tradition of doing things differently where age is concerned; in other cases, necessity (i.e. early retirement of the Current Gen or incapacity) may force the family's hand. From our experience with family businesses, the most prevalent motivation for defying age preconceptions is to level the playing field between Current Gen and Next Gen, in order to take full advantage of the potential contributions of both generations. However common, age preconceptions undermine trust maturity and prevent peer-to-peer collaboration from blossoming. Assuming an individual can't do something because of their age – older or younger – runs directly counter to trust, even if the generations don't make this assumption explicit in word or deed. Without age preconceptions to divide them, the Current Gen and the Next Gen can concentrate on doing what is best for the business and the family.

Enforcing behavioural norms that support collective action, such as mandatory attendance and essential participation, would at first glance appear to run counter to the emphasis on individual self-determination that defying age preconceptions implies. After all, behavioural norms, particularly injunctive behavioural norms of the kind described here, represent limitation and constraint: you have to attend meetings and you must be well prepared.[2]

The very idea of behavioural norms such as these derives from the need for communities to keep individuals and their propensities in check for the good of the whole, but to the detriment of any absolute notion of personal autonomy. On the other hand, in order to gain access to and remain in good standing as members of a community, family members have made a choice to do without certain elements of personal autonomy. In this sense, and however constraining, injunctive behavioural norms may benefit from the strength of voluntary adherence: you follow norms that limit your personal autonomy because you want to.

In practice, it turns out that insisting upon strong behavioural norms is especially important when age preconceptions are done away with, helping to prevent the indiscipline that might ensue if everyone just did their own thing, regardless of age. Indeed, without commonly practised norms of behaviour to regulate how the generations interact, age preconceptions about how individuals from different generations are expected to behave can become self-fulfilling, even with the best of intentions. Without norms for attendance, the Next Gen may be perceived as unreliable, even if they are not predisposed to unreliability; without norms for joint participation, the Current Gen may be perceived to be aloof and autocratic, even if they don't want to be. Contrast these misperceptions with the clear injunction: if you want to be seen as a peer, you had better behave like a peer. Following this line of reasoning, a Middle Eastern family business has taken the unprecedented step of opening up the ownership council to the Next Gen from the age of 30, *provided* that the representatives of the Next Gen demonstrate commitment over time and pass objective hurdles. Again, age preconceptions are defied, yes, but with the proviso of clear expectations from the collective. Balancing age indifference with firmly enforced behavioural norms is not a simple recipe for success, but it does constitute a particularly effective and stable basis on which the generations can work together.

Set outsized challenges and install safety nets (supporting capability appreciation)

Recall the example of the scion of a European machine technology business who is asked to take over and turn around an ailing foreign subsidiary, a tremendous personal and organizational challenge. The possibility of failure is real, but the assignment is embedded in a purpose-built safety net: a) the effort is given board-level support, with senior mentors assigned to back up the Next Gen in his task; and b) there is a clearly defined ceiling for how much money will be invested – the financial risk to the business as a whole is tightly circumscribed. Even if the heir apparent to the family business fails to turn around the ailing subsidiary, he will experience personal growth in the process and the damage to the company will be limited. Unlike in the popular Netflix drama *Succession*, the kind of outsized challenge we are describing here is not meant to throw the Next Gen to the wolves. Safety nets are installed to ensure that the Next Gen has a real chance to demonstrate personal capability, without the perpetual fear of imminent disaster.

The positive relationship between setting outsized challenges and achieving personal and group objectives is well documented in social psychology, and comes under the heading of goal-setting theory.[3] Specifying the importance of a large, concrete goal, this research shows robust results under a variety of conditions, both in the laboratory and in organizational settings. In a family business, setting outsized goals implies the Next Gen taking on projects of critical importance early on, and the Current Gen continuing to aim for ambitious goals rather than slowing down.[4] Free from the influence of outside shareholders, the family business may indeed be a particularly propitious arena for setting outsized challenges, if adequate safety nets are put in place. For the Next Gen, in any case, outsized challenges represent an important proving ground for demonstrating their potential and thus building capability appreciation between the generations. In many cases, the Next Gen itself actively seeks out such challenges within the family business or, just as often, outside the family business, with Next-Gen-run ventures playing an increasingly important role.[5] Like it did for Heracles in Greek mythology (the 12 labours) or Abraham in the Old Testament (the sacrifice of Isaac, Genesis 22:1–19) or the disciples of Jesus in the New Testament (the provision of food for a crowd, Luke 9:12–13), the attempt to complete seemingly impossible tasks can be a critical step in demonstrating that the Next Gen is worthy of the Current Gen's esteem.[6]

Installing safety nets represents the other side of the coin to setting outsized challenges. As an academic concept, the safety net is better known in political economics and development economics than in business, but the idea of offering support and determining a floor for losses is applicable to any kind of complex project.[7] Different challenges require different safety nets, both in terms of resource support and risk limitation as outlined above, but also in terms of making the possibility of failure acceptable. By definition, not every outsized challenge can be successfully met. Outsized challenges that result in objective failure are still good opportunities for learning, not least for learning about and improving the relationship between the Current Gen and the Next Gen. In this sense, it is helpful if the family business is active in multiple areas, providing different opportunities for trying things out. A culture that allows for failure, promotes honest analysis of what may have gone wrong and gives second chances constitutes an essential element of an adequate safety system.

It is worth noting here that setting outsized challenges often goes hand in hand with defying age preconceptions. At the American family conglomerate described above, for example, the youngest Next Gen was entrusted with planning and running a major company project while still in university and without much relevant prior experience. Without a doubt, individual aptitude also plays a major role in making experiences like this one successful. However, even the most capable Next Gen will do better if strong behavioural norms and a purpose-built safety net are in place. In this particular case, the Next Gen could draw upon the well-developed meeting culture of the family and the generous mentoring of non-family executives to bring the project home.

Empower freedom of choice and assign responsibilities (supporting role respect)

Earlier, we described the unusual career path of the founder of a Swiss medical business who entrusts the family jewels to his son and, rather than continuing to oversee his baby (pun intended) from the chair, moves on to a new venture. What does this account illustrate? From a traditional succession perspective, the founder's move out of the legacy business corresponds to the tenets of good governance, promoting a clean separation of ownership and control (cf. Chapter 9). At a deeper level, however, the move is about the founder and his son both seizing the freedom to fulfil their personal potential, the first as a serial entrepreneur, the second as a fully fledged CEO. Many family businesses pay lip service to freedom of choice – free to join or not join, free to decide where to work, free to seek the top spot and free to quit on your own terms – but, in fact, true freedom of choice is not that common in family businesses. Notwithstanding policies and statements to the contrary, there are often strong pressures to join the family business (see Chapter 2); in some cases, there are limits on the range of positions available to family members, and clearly defined restrictions on occupying the top spot; in most family businesses, shareholding agreements raise barriers to individuals making a clean exit. In other words, where the family business is concerned, family members often find themselves with very little room to manoeuvre. What is most striking in the example of the Swiss medical business described above is the freedom of choice to make their own career decisions enjoyed by *both* the father and the son.

Freedom of choice is a key idea in economics and in politics (going back to Aristotle).[8] In his famous treatise on the subject, Amartya Sen stresses the intrinsic value of freedom of choice, over the purely instrumental (i.e. as a means to an end) and argues that freedom of choice can be seen as an inherently positive concept (freedom *to do* something, as opposed to freedom as the absence of constraints). Aristotle and Sen explain the importance of freedom of choice in the context of the polity and political association, but freedom of choice is in fact fundamental to every aspect of modern life: freedom to choose whom to marry, whether or not to have children, where to live and how to spend time. Imagine the contrary and you quickly find yourself back in the most restrictive societies of the Middle Ages, where personal freedoms were tightly circumscribed by caste, belief, profession and many other constraints related to who you were born as, rather than who you wanted to be. Theoretically, the members of a family business have the freedom of choice to do anything they want, more freedom, in fact, than most other people, when measured in terms of financial capacity and the sheer variety of choices available to them by virtue of their position. In reality, as we have seen, their freedom is often severely restricted: by obligation, by duty, by history and by the older generation(s) looking over their shoulders. It's not the Middle Ages, but it is often a golden cage of constraints. The de facto absence of personal freedom, then, is why freedom of choice becomes an especially strong leadership practice in family business, not just for the Next Gen, but also for the Current Gen.

In the ideal case and as exemplified by the Swiss medical business, individual freedom of choice is balanced with clearly assigned responsibilities with respect to the group. Thus, jobs are accurately spelled out, both in day-to-day operations and in governance; there are clear lines of authority and objective standards in place to measure performance and reward achievement; and career advancement is rigorously formalized. These are the necessary means to ensure cohesion, to prevent people from running off in different directions where the business is concerned, when freedom of choice is a way of life in the family. The alternative is confusion over who is in charge and what is expected – not only in the family but also, just as importantly, among non-family employees. In the family business, freedom of choice implies voluntary commitment to the greater good, each according to his/her abilities and inclinations. Assigned responsibilities represent the flip-side of this freedom, adapted to the functions that family members choose to pursue.

Assigned responsibilities (within a system of governance) are mentioned by many authors as critical to having a successful, long-lived family business,[9] but freedom of choice, its counterpart in our analysis, does not merit similar consideration. In our research, it is precisely the combination of sincere freedom of choice and clear responsibility assignment that builds role respect. Again, we have yin and yang, sometimes simultaneous, other times overlapping or sequential in time. Recall from Part Three that both the Current Gen and the Next Gen have a specific role to play in the life of the family business, the current as a guarantor of stability, the next as a catalyst for the future. Without freedom of choice, family members, particularly of the Next Gen, will not commit wholeheartedly and may even withdraw entirely; without assigned responsibilities, family members will not fulfil their respective roles effectively.

Applying the leadership practices over time

From the examples discussed above, it might seem that defying age preconceptions and its counterpart, enforcing behavioural norms, are leadership practices aimed primarily at the early phase of the transition between the generations, when they are first learning to work side by side, while setting outsized challenges/installing safety nets and enabling freedom of choice/assigning responsibilities come later in the process, towards the middle and late stages, when succession is in the air. In fact, all three pairs can be used throughout the transition, separately and together. Part of the difficulty in thinking about the transition process in terms of orderly, clearly defined stages comes from the evidence on the ground: different families do things differently in terms of timing and scope. While it is possible to speak of early, middle and late stages of transition between the generations, it is not meaningful to assign averages for duration or extent, there is simply too much variation. Thus, in some families the Next Gen is entrusted with very large projects at a young age, while in other families the Current Gen holds on to supreme command de facto, even after the baton has formally passed to the Next Gen. What we can say is that we observe the use of all three leadership practice pairs at every stage of the Current and Next Gens' collaboration with each other, but to varying degrees, depending on the requirements of the situation.

Early on, typically when the Next Gen takes a serious adult interest in the family business (i.e. first full employment or first formal role), age preconceptions and outsized challenges may play a predominant role, but freedom of choice in combination with assigned responsibilities is also put to use. Consider the following example, observed across multiple business families, in which the Next Gen is called upon or itself asks to work on governance questions. Either way, freedom of choice is at work, both in how the Next Gen takes on the task and in the governance recommendations they come up with. Thus, when the twenty-somethings of a fifth-generation European business family were entrusted with reviewing and future proofing the existing governance arrangements, they developed their own way of collaborating and made sure that the revised governance structure included alternative, but equally viable, paths for family members to contribute to the business. Assigned responsibilities, in turn, were central to both how the Next Gen and the Current Gen interacted on the project and what kind of governance recommendations they came up with. Needless to say at this point, the whole idea of entrusting such an important piece of work to the Next Gen so early in their business lives defied age preconceptions and set an outsized challenge.

All of the transformation initiatives presented in the introduction to this book can be classified as fitting into the middle period of the Next Gen's side-by-side collaboration with the Current Gen: the two generations have already worked together for a number of years and have built up a track record, both shared and individual. Despite the existence of track records, we find that setting outsized challenges continues to have an important function, as proving ground and as motivation. Towards the middle of the transition between the generations, the Next Gen might be asked to take on a much bigger job than before, i.e. running a foreign subsidiary as above, or becoming the CEO of a division. If this is the case, and especially if this happens at a relatively young age, avoiding interference (enforcing the Current Gen's adherence to mutually agreed behavioural norms) is an additional critical factor, over and above the installation of safety nets. The Current Gen who hands out a big challenge to the Next Gen, but cannot avoid interfering or going behind the Next Gen's back to clean up mistakes, is putting the outcome of the transition process in danger. Whether it be a particular job or a transformation initiative, the challenge has a better chance of succeeding if the generations have found an effective way of working together.

Once the generations have entered a later stage of the transition, when the Current Gen can see themselves handing over the baton or indeed have already handed over and are watching over the Next Gen, behavioural norms and safety nets will most likely be (or should be) well established. At this point, freedom of choice and clear-cut assignments may take centre stage. Will the retired founder who is still the majority shareholder allow the Next Gen's decision to exit the legacy business to stand? This was the key question faced by two generations of a northern European vehicle importer, when push came to shove about strategy. Or is the new authority of the Next Gen who have taken over the reins sufficiently well accepted so that senior non-family employees do not feel the need to ask for permission from the previous CEO/now chair? This was the difficulty at a Swiss processed foods manufacturer that had formally completed the succession process but had not done enough to assign and clarify responsibilities. In general, then, the leadership practices we have identified as central to supporting trust maturity, capability appreciation and role respect find application throughout the transition process between the generations, in a more or less pronounced manner. Critically, ignoring or, worse, acting contrary to these leadership practices undermines side-by-side collaboration and puts a smooth transition between the generations at risk.

Maintaining dynamic tension and finding the right combination of leadership practices

Just because the generations have been working together for a long time and the Current Gen is at the chronological point of wanting to hand does not imply that Current Gen and Next Gen have got the balance right between individual self-determination and collective discipline. In the best case, the swings in emphasis between the two types of paired leadership practices get smaller over time, so that the dynamic tension of yin and yang is in a state of equilibrium. This is what learning over time is supposed to achieve. As the swings become smaller, trust maturity (related to preconceptions/norms), capability appreciation (related to challenges/safety nets) and role respect (related to freedom/responsibilities) grow (see Figure 10.1). However, it is never good to assume smooth sailing. Perhaps the best way to think about managing the balance between individual self-determination and collective discipline is to liken the process to a walk on a tightrope. Neither the Current Gen nor the Next Gen can afford to stop paying attention and watching their steps.

As indicated above, we often find the three pairs of leadership practices applied together, or in various combinations of two. In fact, they work best together, not in isolation, because one reinforces the other: thus, at the individual level, setting outsized challenges makes defiance of age preconceptions

Figure 10.1 Navigating the transition: Leadership practices

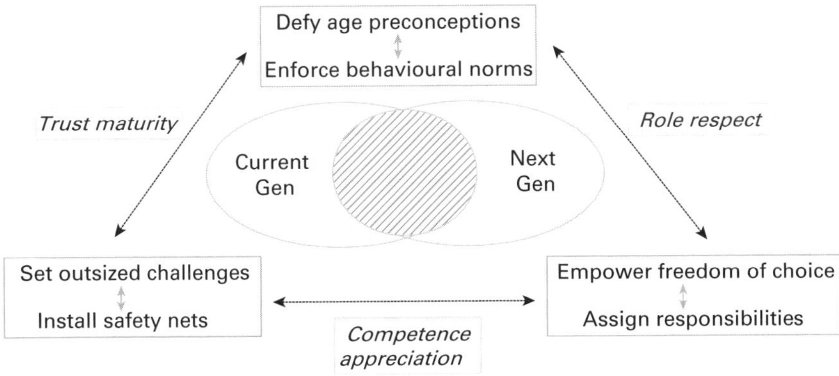

concrete – action and not just talk; empowering freedom of choice keeps outsized challenges intrinsically motivated – aspiration and not merely obligation; and defying age conceptions paves the road for true freedom of choice – custom made and not rule driven. Employed together, defying age preconceptions, setting outsized challenges and empowering freedom of choice make the transition between the generations real and put the onus on the individual family member to take responsibility and live up to his/her potential. Analogously, enforcing behavioural norms, installing safety nets and assigning responsibilities go hand in hand to maintain high-quality execution at a collective level. High-quality execution, in turn, is important to ensure that the generational transition process does not damage the business or the family. Nonetheless, not all families transitioning to peer-based collaboration apply all three pairs of leadership practices in conjunction; each family finds its own combination, according to its position on the 'hierarchical to peer-based relations' continuum between the generations, its stage of evolution in the succession process and its specific needs for leadership and governance.

KEY TAKEAWAYS

1. Successful generational transition employs a distinctive set of leadership practices.
2. Balancing the individual and aspirational with the collective and foundational is critical.
3. Every family finds its own specific approach, depending on the business and the people.

Learning journey: Pit stop 10

Please refer to Chapter 12 for a full explanation of the educational approach supporting the learning journey.

SELF-LEARNING

Self-assessment

Assess where your family is and should be on the continua between:

'Defy age preconceptions' and 'Enforce behavioural norms'

'Set outsized challenges' and 'Install safety nets'

'Empower freedom of choice' and 'Assign responsibilities'

Development plan for Current Gen/Next Gen

Draw up a development plan in which you define the following milestones:

Short term: What will I do by next week to close the leadership practice gap? What will I consider a success by then?

Medium term: What will I do by next month to close the leadership practice gap? What will I consider a success by then?

Long term: What will I do by next year to close the leadership practice gap? What will I consider a success by then?

Action review

Mark the dates in your calendar when you check how well you have achieved the short-, medium- and long-term goals you set. Evaluate what you have achieved and look back at what went well and what went poorly.

MODERATED WORKSHOP LEARNING

Group discussion

Use the material presented in Chapter 10 as a launch pad for thinking about and critically discussing how your family business applies the leadership practices described in this book.

How well does your family strike a balance between:

'Defy age preconceptions' and 'Enforce behavioural norms'

'Set outsized challenges' and 'Install safety nets'

'Empower freedom of choice' and 'Assign responsibilities'

What hinders your family business from finding the right balance between:

'Defy age preconceptions' and 'Enforce behavioural norms'

'Set outsized challenges' and 'Install safety nets'

'Empower freedom of choice' and 'Assign responsibilities'

What can your family business do to strike a better balance between:

'Defy age preconceptions' and 'Enforce behavioural norms'

'Set outsized challenges' and 'Install safety nets'

'Empower freedom of choice' and 'Assign responsibilities'

Development plan for Current Gen/Next Gen

Draw up a development plan in which you define the following milestones:

Short term: What will I do by next week to close the leadership practice gap? What will I consider a success by then?

Medium term: What will I do by next month to close the leadership practice gap? What will I consider a success by then?

Long term: What will I do by next year to close the leadership practice gap? What will I consider a success by then?

Co-coaching

Choose a member of another family and share your development plan with him or her. Arrange two follow-up meetings after two months and after six months to see how well you have implemented your plan.

CLASSROOM LEARNING

Group discussion

Use the material presented in Chapter 10 as a launch pad for thinking about and critically discussing how family businesses apply the leadership practices described in this book.

What conditions help family businesses strike a balance between:

'Defy age preconceptions' and 'Enforce behavioural norms'

'Set outsized challenges' and 'Install safety nets'

'Empower freedom of choice' and 'Assign responsibilities'

What hinders family businesses from finding the right balance between:

'Defy age preconceptions' and 'Enforce behavioural norms'

'Set outsized challenges' and 'Install safety nets'

'Empower freedom of choice' and 'Assign responsibilities'

What can family businesses do to strike a better balance between:

'Defy age preconceptions' and 'Enforce behavioural norms'

'Set outsized challenges' and 'Install safety nets'

'Empower freedom of choice' and 'Assign responsibilities'

Oxford-style debate

Form two teams and prepare to debate the following thesis, with one team in favour and the other team against:

Everybody in the family can be a leader and learn how to apply the appropriate leadership practices.

Conduct a debate to collect all possible and valid arguments for and against the proposal.

Case report

Choose a family business that you know or are familiar with and analyse how they apply the three leadership practice pairs. Make concrete suggestions on how to further improve their leadership.

11 Transformation initiatives

Launch, build momentum, embed and conclude

We assume that the readers of this book – Current Gen and Next Gen, colleagues and advisers – want to put what they have learned into practice. As we have emphasized from the outset, transformation initiatives in strategy, sustainability and governance represent a particularly effective vehicle for testing and improving the ability of the generations to work together for the good of the family business. What makes for a successful transformation initiative? In our research and advisory experience with family businesses around the world, it helps to think of a transformation initiative in terms of four successive and interlinked phases: how to launch a transformation, how to maintain momentum, how to embed a transformation in the organization and, finally, how to conclude a transformation.[1] Whatever the objective of the transformation, each of the four phases calls for distinct, specially adapted processes (see Figure 11.1).

In this chapter, we offer specific advice for how to carry out a side-by-side transformation initiative in the family business, from launch through to conclusion. What aspects of our advice are most relevant to you depends on where you are in the timeline of running such a transformation initiative. In any case, and even if no transformation initiative has yet been attempted, it is never too late to consider a transformation that reflects the lessons presented in this book. For the sake of immediacy, we address the following practical recommendations directly to the family business reader.

Figure 11.1 The life cycle of a transformation initiative

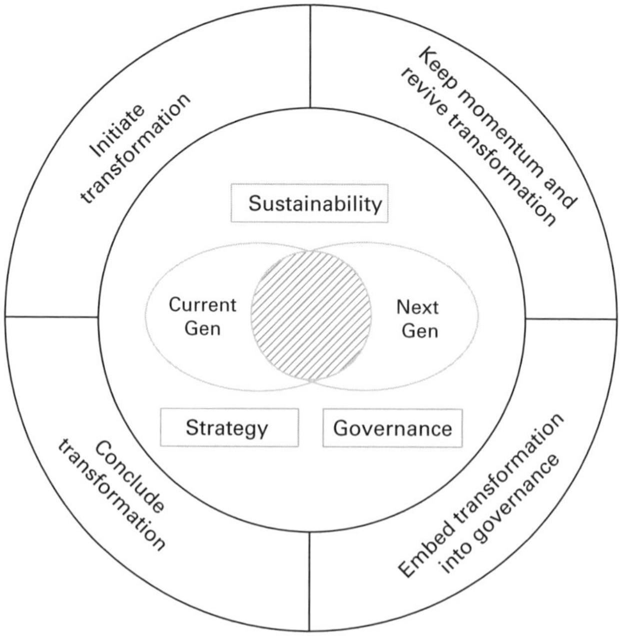

How to launch a transformation

If you and your family have not yet begun to work on transformation of the kind described in this book, the first question you should ask yourself is whether it is even necessary to do so. While the desire for transformative change, in terms of strategy, sustainability or governance, can be very strong, especially in the Next Gen, desire alone is not enough to justify the hard work and upheaval that a transformation initiative necessarily entails. Three baseline conditions must be met to justify the launching of a transformation initiative:

1 **Family capacity for a transformation initiative:** The first condition for launching a successful transformation initiative is the right constellation of family members across generations, covering the appropriate mix of expertise and experience, coupled with the potential and desire to develop further required skills over time. Family capacity for a transformation initiative is closely tied to what we talked about in terms of capability appreciation in Part Two. Without mutual capability appreciation, there is a strong possibility that a transformation initiative

gets derailed quickly – not because of an actual lack of skills in the family but because of a failure on the part of the Current Gen and the Next Gen to recognize that the required capabilities are in fact available.

2 **Family readiness for a transformation initiative:** Over and above family capacity for transformation, it is necessary to take a hard look at whether family members, both those who are actively involved and those along for the ride in a passive way, are willing to engage in the transformation initiative and live up to their roles and responsibilities. Critical to assessing a family's readiness for transformation is timing. Even if the skills are there in theory, people have to be ready and willing to take time away from their daily activities and get involved in the transformation initiative – a half-hearted attempt will not go anywhere and will leave both the Current Gen and the Next Gen unwilling to attempt similar efforts in the future.

3 **The business case for the transformation initiative:** A successful transformation initiative serves the family *and* adds value to the family business. Therefore, a strong business case is an absolute necessity. A strong business case helps gain acceptance and reinforces credibility, not only in the family but also with non-family business leaders. Fundamentally, the kind of transformation initiatives we are discussing here will have a lasting effect both on the principal business of the family and on the way it does business. When assessing the business case for the transformation initiative, therefore, it is important to consider the broader, long-term impact and include hard-to-measure elements such as economic optionality (for strategic innovation initiatives) or risk reduction (for sustainability and governance initiatives).

Once family capacity and readiness are ascertained and the business case is established, it is important to involve the right people in the appropriate way to create the conditions for success. Experience shows that while it is critical to keep everyone in the loop, it is also important to be discerning in how to involve different stakeholders. As the term 'family business' implies, there are several types of players to consider:

- *Family members of the Current Gen active in the business:* Central to strategy, sustainability and governance in place, the active Current Gen takes a leading role in any transformation initiative.
- *Family members of the Next Gen active in the business:* A successful transformation initiative always involves active Next Gens in leading roles, *alongside* and together with active Current Gens.

- *Passive Current Gen family members:* Family members who do not play an active role in the family business and do not aspire to do so may still have an important function (i.e. as branch representative), making it very useful to consider their advice.
- *Passive Next Gen family members:* Even if passive Next Gens cannot currently imagine playing an active role in the family business, their stance may change over time. Therefore, keeping them informed is good practice.
- *Non-family executives and non-family board members in the family business:* Even if they never become shareholders, non-family individuals typically play a crucial role in creating economic value for the business and will want to be informed and consulted.
- *Independent family business consultant/facilitator:* Given the many, sometimes conflicting, interests and stakes involved in launching a transformation initiative, an independent coach can be a very useful resource.

Successfully launching a transformation initiative requires clear direction and shared leadership from at least a few active family members across the different generations, and proactive involvement from passive family members as well as non-family business leaders. Ideally, all of the relevant stakeholders mentioned here are included, in different capacities and at different times, according to their skills and motivations.

COMPANY HISTORY 1

The case of a European family that owns a leading niche healthcare company in the 5th generation illustrates the successful launch of a transformation initiative that started as a governance and succession planning exercise and eventually involved strategy and organization.

In order to better understand the case, a little bit of context is useful. First, it is important to note that the family had already set up a family constitution that established the flow of information between management, the board and the family council, and defined decision-making processes within and among the different bodies. Furthermore, the practice of family members holding several meetings per year with non-family business leaders to get first-hand information about company strategy and performance was well established. In other words, the family had a habit of learning about company issues and being consulted on questions of governance and strategy.

To launch the governance transformation initiative, the two brothers of the Current Gen who were running the business and felt it was time to seriously consider their own succession convened the family council, composed of all family members. In a first step, the family members discussed the upcoming strategic challenges and the implications for the future management model and its leadership. In a second step, all family members were asked to express their desire for and interest in taking an active role in the family business. The results of this survey and the transformation timeline were openly shared with non-family management and the board of directors to get their inputs. The open discussion led to a clear understanding that, of the five cousins, one was interested and could envision taking an active role in the family business because of his family background, three preferred to become active owners, while one wanted to sell his shares. Although it took considerably longer than a traditional top-down approach, transparency and the inclusion of non-family stakeholders under the determined leadership of the Current Gen got this initiative off to a strong and sustainable start.

How to build momentum (and revive a stalled transformation initiative)

A transformation initiative can take longer than expected and follow a trajectory that is difficult to predict. As interests shift and business conditions change, even the most carefully structured plans may need to be adjusted, leading to revised timelines. Particularly if it is a first-time experience for the Current and the Next Gens to work together on a major undertaking, the process is likely to bear surprises and can lead to disappointments. It is important, therefore, to devise ways to maintain momentum and overcome the challenges that are typical of these kinds of initiatives.

The first sign that a process is in danger of stalling is a lack of progress; a lack of progress, in turn, is likely to lead to transformation fatigue. Thus, participants may waver in their belief that the desired outcome can be achieved, or may simply lose interest. If this happens, they are likely to feel tired of talking and begin to question the process. If not addressed proactively, transformation fatigue can lead to open conflict over goals and process management. These conflicts can turn into personal disputes, with some family members accusing others of putting their own interests ahead of the interests of the business, if they are not addressed up front. At that stage, it is very difficult to salvage the process and starting over may be the only way forward. How can you stay on top of things and recognize early warning signs of stalling?

In our experience, stalling of the transformation initiative can be prevented by incorporating an information framework that follows four key rules:

1. *Recognize and communicate quick wins:* Even though the entire process often takes several years, it is important to achieve visible results early in the process to signal to all stakeholders that something is changing for the better.
2. *Be transparent and honest in sharing information:* In order to maintain trust, it is essential to keep all stakeholders fully informed, and also to share bad news so that solutions for overcoming challenges can be discussed.
3. *Institutionalize the decision-making process:* To ensure stability and predictability in the transformation process, decision-making must be institutionalized. Family councils or conventions, in combination with family constitutions or strategies, are common methods for creating effective mechanisms for making decisions that are accepted by all stakeholders.
4. *Reaffirm regularly shared commitments:* Most important, however, is to constantly ensure that the various endeavours are aligned and that potential conflicts can be identified early and addressed proactively.

The 5th generation healthcare family business described above consistently followed this approach. Not only was it very diligent in initiating the transition process, it was also very disciplined in adopting a more formal approach that at times seemed almost bureaucratic, but ultimately proved to be very successful. Regular meetings of the family council served to inform not only about the transformation per se, but also business development and leadership issues. The achievement of key milestones was celebrated and used to test the commitment and agreement of all involved. This allowed for potential challenges to be highlighted and proactive countermeasures to be taken. Figure 11.2 maps the ups and downs typical of this kind of change process.

Figure 11.2 Monitoring the progress of a transformation initiative

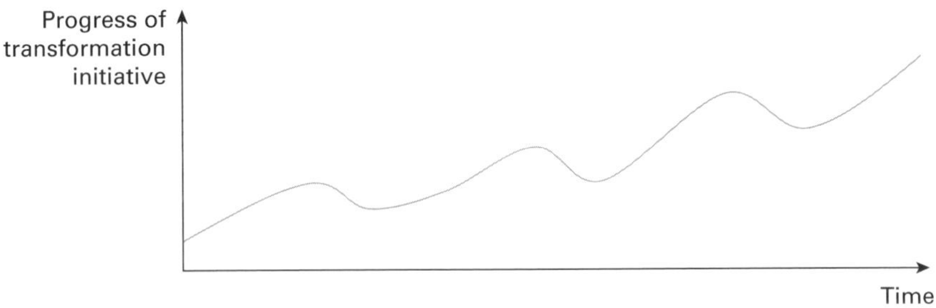

Even with the best intentions and an adequate information framework in place, there is always a risk that the process of transformation will slow down to the point of frustration. In this case, what can be done?

1. *Get an independent voice involved in the process:* Since disruptions to a transition initiative are often the result of different and conflicting interests, it can be helpful to bring in an independent voice to try to help break any impasse.
2. *Understand the root cause:* In order to find solutions, it is important to fully understand the root causes of the slowdown. Is the breakdown due to lack of commitment, lack of alignment or lack of performance?
3. *Recalibrate the process:* If the root cause is a lack of engagement or a misalignment of people, the process needs to be paused and adjusted so that all parties can be brought on board. If, on the other hand, inadequate performance is identified as the problem, personnel changes may be required. Either way, the original plan needs to be adjusted.
4. *Separate personal and professional issues:* Throughout the process and as hard as this can be in the context of family relationships, it is important to remind participants in the transformation initiative to separate professional issues from personal considerations in looking for solutions.

COMPANY HISTORY 2

The case of a European industrial family business in the 5th generation illustrates the value of such intervention mechanisms. What began as an initiative to reshape the company's governance soon developed into a dispute over the group's future strategy. The starting point was a seemingly orderly succession process in a diversified group with four different business units. The father, in his late sixties, was keen to pass the business on to the Next Gen. His two children were accomplished academics with doctorates in their fields. They were interested and willing to serve on the board, but did not see their future in an operational role in the company. The son, however, was willing to take over the role of chair of the board of directors from his father and serve as what he called an active chair.

The family initiated a transition process in which the Current and Next Gens agreed to a gradual handover. They hired an external consultant to support the son in the background and reassure the father that everything was in good hands. At the same time, all other stakeholders in the family and the company were regularly informed and consulted. Everything seemed to be off to a good start. But while the family-led transition went according to plan, the company's performance faltered. A diversified company that had always generated steady profits to ensure continuous dividend payments began to make losses. While the situation was initially explained as a cyclical problem, the family eventually had the courage to recognize the challenges for what they were: a structural problem closely tied to the transition process. It turned out that the root cause of faltering business performance was a power struggle between non-family business leaders who held fundamentally opposing views about the strategy of the company. Some managers, aware of the impending transition, tried to use the opportunity to impose their ideas about a fundamental reorientation of the company. They believed that the company should focus on the most promising businesses and forget about the others. Another group, trying to take the family's perspective into account, argued that a diversified company was in the best interest of the family. Once this power struggle was recognized, the family, still very focused on and committed to the leadership transition, was able to make the necessary decisions and address the structural issues up front. They brought in an outside consultant to help them review the ownership policy and the business strategy. This helped bring the debate back to a factual level and address some of the underlying issues that had led to turmoil.

How to embed a transformation (in the organization)

To ensure the long-term viability of a transformation initiative, the results should be institutionalized and integrated into the existing governance structures. At the same time, the transformation initiative should be treated as a project distinct from the routine affairs of the family and the family business. This dilemma requires a very deliberate approach to reviewing and possibly adjusting governance structures as the initiative unfolds.

A methodical approach is required. We suggest that families consider the following four steps:

1. *Review the ownership and governance model:* Transformation initiatives in strategy, sustainability and governance present an opportunity to review the current ownership structure to reflect upon future viability. Do all family members still see themselves as committed owners? Does the ownership structure offer sufficient incentives to align the interests of future business leaders, whether they come from the family or not? Does the future strategy require additional capital? If so, where will the capital come from? Answers to all of these questions contribute to making a major transformation initiative sustainable.
2. *Choose the right leaders:* Transformation only has an enduring effect if it is led by the right people. Therefore, the composition of the various boards and governance bodies may need to be reconsidered. This applies to both family members and non-family members alike. It is important to take a long-term perspective and, in particular, to assess the readiness and career paths of future leaders. Who will one day play a central role in leading the family and the company into the future? How can future leaders be developed?
3. *Establish a road map:* A clear road map ensures that long-term plans can be put into action. In this context, the right sequence of steps is required. This is highly dependent on the leadership pipeline and its readiness. Developing such a road map therefore requires someone who not only understands the future strategies of the family and the business but is also familiar with the various leaders, both internal and external to the family, who will one day assume a leadership role. These can be respected family members or independent advisers who have credibility with all stakeholders.

4 *Live the new strategy/sustainability/governance model:* Most importantly, all stakeholders must begin to live the new model. This involves not only a deliberate people selection process, but also an onboarding process. New leaders need to be well prepared and introduced to their new roles. This is particularly important to ensure that all leaders, both internal and external to the family, who become involved in the management of the business fully understand the heritage, culture and strategy of the family and the business. Figure 11.3 illustrates the transition from initiative-led to institutionalized transformation.

Figure 11.3 From initiative-led transformation to institutionalized transformation

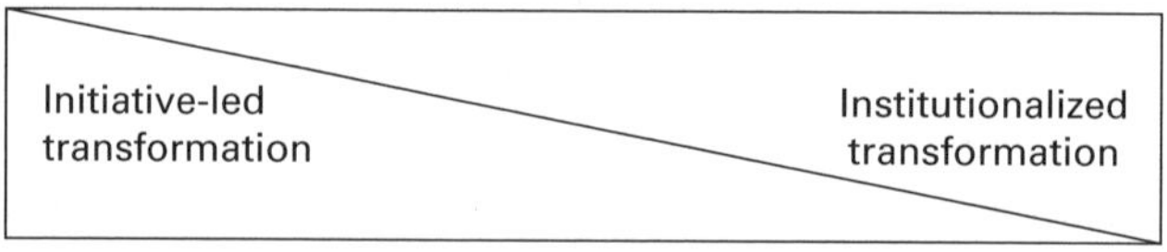

COMPANY HISTORY 3

The case of a family that runs a global machinery business in the 5th generation illustrates how the results of a transformation initiative can be effectively embedded in the structure of the organization. The company, which has grown from a small workshop in the mid-19th century to a global player that is the market leader in its machine segment and develops and produces machines for the world's leading manufacturing companies, has always been family-owned. There has never been a question as to whether the family is the best owner. When the father, who was CEO and chair of the board of directors, asked his only son if he could imagine replacing him one day, the son was very unsure. He had just graduated from business school and wanted to explore the world. Both agreed that he should first explore the industry and the world in another company. The father was able to get his son a job as an assistant to the CEO of one of his clients, a well-known and successful manufacturer. What the son didn't know at the time was that the father had asked the CEO, a respected business partner, to give his son particularly difficult tasks to test his readiness. For the father, it was not just about the son exploring his options, but also about testing his abilities for a future leadership role in the family business. The son not only completed the tasks with flying colours, but also discovered his liking for the industry. Subsequently, the two agreed on a well-planned transition process in which the son took on various positions in the family business to learn about all areas of the company, eventually assuming the position of managing director while his father continued as chairman of the board.

As the son learned more about the company and the industry, he found that, although the company continued to perform well, the industry landscape was changing rapidly as some competitors merged and new competitors emerged from Asia. Looking at comparable industries, he concluded that the industry was facing consolidation, and he was determined to play an active role in that process. He also recognized that, as a family business, they would not have the financial clout of some of their competitors. He suggested they explore all options, including merging with a competitor or going public to raise capital for a possible acquisition. The father acknowledged the need for action but was less convinced by the proposed options. To find a way out of the impasse, he turned to an old friend and business partner, the CEO of another family business that had just gone public, maintaining the family's position of power as an anchor investor. The three of them discussed all the options and eventually concluded that an initial public offering (IPO) while keeping the family as a strong anchor investor was the right way to play an active role in the expected period of industry consolidation.

Based on the proven playbook of the family friend, they designed and launched a transformation initiative to make the company ready for the IPO, and developed a governance structure that would satisfy both the interests of the future external shareholders and the family as the main owner. They decided to propose the family friend as the future chair of the board of directors, given his track record of successfully transforming a family business, and to propose the father as a member of the board to ensure continuity, while the son would continue leading the company into the future as CEO. In addition, a number of new independent directors were proposed to join the board. These changes in the management structure not only provided excellent conditions for a successful implementation of the IPO plan, but were also very well received by potential investors approached in preparation for the IPO. The future investors considered this to be an ideal mix of talent, demonstrating the family commitment and independent perspectives necessary for effective corporate governance. The IPO was over-subscribed several times and the structure proved successful in further strengthening the company's position in the market. At the same time, the proceeds from the IPO not only helped to increase the company's financial clout, but also enabled the family to manage its legacy and diversify the family assets.

How to conclude a transformation

Every transformation initiative has an end point. This distinguishes initiatives and projects from regular operations. Acknowledging the end date of a transformation initiative is crucial for two main reasons. First, initiatives are always an additional burden for those involved, from which they must be relieved after a certain period of time. Second, at some point, the moment of truth arrives and it is time to assess whether the efforts have lived up to expectations.

Bringing a transformation initiative to a successful conclusion requires a number of explicit measures:

1 *Define success to determine when the final milestone is reached:* While every transformation initiative begins with goals in mind, determining when these objectives have been met usually varies widely. Therefore, it is critical to clearly define what success means and remind all stakeholders of this definition on a regular basis.

2 *Celebrate the conclusion of the transformation initiative:* Once the mutually agreed final milestone has been reached, it is time to celebrate success. This can be done as part of a formal celebration, such as a family jubilee or the retirement of a family business leader, and is often accompanied by a communications campaign to inform all stakeholders of what has been achieved. The signalling effect of such a celebration is important not only for family members, but especially for non-family members who may not have been as closely involved in the initiative but need to know about the changes in strategy, sustainability or governance.

3 *Learn from successes and failures in the transformation process:* The celebratory mode should not overshadow the necessary learning. As we have seen, a transformation initiative always goes through ups and downs. People make mistakes, but they also recover from them. It is helpful to review the process and develop an open perspective on what went well, and what went poorly. This is where it can be helpful to bring in an independent consultant who can make an objective assessment without blaming individuals.

4 *Write a transformation playbook with and for future generations:* Talking only about successes and failures would be a missed opportunity. Since future generations are likely to face similar transformation challenges,

families are well advised to use the outcomes of the initiative review process to write a transformation playbook. This also provides a perfect opportunity to include multiple generations – the current, the next and, if they are old enough, even some members of the future (next-next) generation that is likely to play an important role in transformations to come. Developing such a playbook can prove to be a very valuable learning journey for all those involved and improves the chances of making a success of future transformations (see Figure 11.4).

Figure 11.4 Writing a transformation playbook

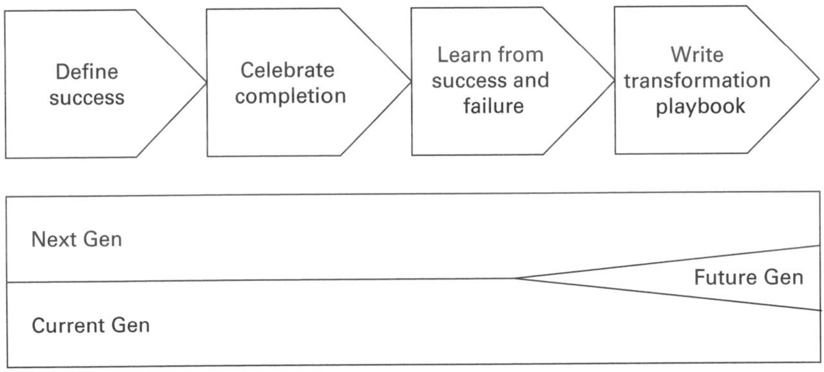

COMPANY HISTORY 4

The history of a second-generation family that owns a successful medical technology business provides a vivid example of how to successfully complete a transformation initiative, in this example an initiative focused on sustainability. The history of this family business starts with two brothers, who founded a company that became a global leader in its field. Success attracted the interest of a leading multinational company that eventually made the brothers a multi-billion dollar offer to acquire the company. In the sale talks with the suitor and his own brother, the older brother was able to retain one business unit for himself and his branch of the family, a unit that was developing a new group of products that had not yet been launched and was of no interest to the buyer.

Instead of simply enjoying his accumulated wealth, the older brother took the new company to new heights and eventually took it public, retaining a majority stake. One reason for his second run at starting and growing a business was that the succession seemed assured: one of his sons had committed himself early on to following in his footsteps. Instead of simply leaving a lot of money, the older brother wanted to pass on a company to the Next Gen. After successful stints in management positions outside the family business, the son joined the family company and eventually became CEO, while his father remained chair.

Next to his interest in the company and the industry, the son developed a strong passion for a topic that would soon have a major impact on the company's strategy: sustainability. Influenced also by his wife, who was a passionate ecologist and very committed to the preservation of nature, he always believed that business had a special responsibility to protect and preserve nature, something his father was less concerned about. The son was determined to make the company he ran a beacon of sustainable business. Well aware that some of his father's generation, many of whom sat on the company's board of directors, still needed to be convinced of the benefits of sustainability, he and his team developed a proposal for making sustainability a major focus for all of the company's activities and processes, had it approved by the board and then set out to implement it.

The transformation initiative was communicated throughout the company, as well as to all family members, milestones were celebrated, failures were analysed and lessons learned. These reflections were not limited to the boundaries of the company. The company joined several networks and organizations to share and learn from other companies. The son frequently appeared as a speaker at conferences and shared his experiences of successful sustainability transformation. The resounding feedback from external stakeholders, whether investors or clients, convinced even the last sceptics on the board, including the father, that the company was on the right track and well prepared for the next Next Gen.

Side-by-side transformation initiatives in the family business: Final remarks

We have argued that it is useful to consider a transformation initiative in terms of four successive and interlinked phases: how to launch a transformation, how to maintain momentum, how to embed a transformation in the organization and, finally, how to conclude a transformation. Whatever the objective of the transformation – strategy, sustainability or governance – each of the four phases calls for distinct, specially adapted processes. In all of the successful cases we have observed, where transformations have been actually embedded in the organization and concluded, it took persistence and a commitment from both the Current Gen and the Next Gen to be in on the initiative for the long haul. That is not to say that all of the important family and non-family stakeholders had to agree or commit from the outset. Like any other major organizational change project, side-by-side transformation initiatives live or die by the drive and energy of a few individuals. In our experience, initial excitement is easy to come by: if they are recognized as the leaders of the initiative, the Next Gen will start to work with great verve and the Current Gen will be pleased at their offspring's dedication to improving the family asset. The principal threat and the main issue we have observed with transformation initiatives that get stuck in the process is creeping separation from the actual business. If the initiative comes to be seen as separate from the business of doing business, i.e. producing and selling what the family produces and sells, most of the stakeholders eventually lose interest. With all of the concepts and tools presented in this chapter, then, the key thing to bear in mind is to keep the transformation initiative close to the heart of the business.

KEY TAKEAWAYS

1. Transformation initiatives are an important testing arena for side-by-side collaboration.
2. Transformation initiatives follow a life cycle of their own and require specific attention.
3. Embedding transformation initiatives in the business lays the groundwork for change.

Learning journey: Pit stop 11

Please refer to Chapter 12 for a full explanation of the educational approach supporting the learning journey.

SELF-LEARNING

Self-assessment

Determine at what transformation stage your family is:

Launch a transformation

Maintain momentum (and revive a stalled transformation initiative)

Embed a transformation

Conclude a transformation

Assess where your family is and should be when it comes to

The readiness for transformation

The capacity to carry out transformation

Development plan for Current Gen/Next Gen

Draw up a development plan in which you define the following milestones:

Short term: What will I do by next week to close the transformation gap? What will I consider a success by then?

Medium term: What will I do by next month to close the transformation gap? What will I consider a success by then?

Long term: What will I do by next year to close the transformation gap? What will I consider a success by then?

Action review

Mark the dates in your calendar when you check how well you have achieved the short-, medium- and long-term goals you set. Evaluate what you have achieved and look back at what went well and what went poorly.

MODERATED WORKSHOP LEARNING

Case discussion

Read company history 1 and discuss the following questions:

How did the family structure prepare and initiate the process of business transformation and generational change?

What was the role of inclusiveness, i.e. the involvement of all family members, in the process?

Read company history 2 and discuss the following questions:

How did the family use an age-related leadership transition to reinvigorate a much-needed business transformation?

What role did communication play in maintaining the momentum of this business transformation?

Read company history 3 and discuss the following questions:

How did the family use the IPO to transform the business and transition at the same time?

What can we learn from this case about successfully embedding transformation in a family business?

Read company history 4 and discuss the following questions:

How did the father and son manage to find different yet complementary paths in the transition to corporate management?

How did they mark the various milestones in the transformation process, including the final phase?

Development plan for Current Gen/Next Gen

Draw up a development plan in which you define the following milestones:

Short term: What will I do by next week to close the transformation gap? What will I consider a success by then?

Medium term: What will I do by next month to close the transformation gap? What will I consider a success by then?

Long term: What will I do by next year to close the transformation gap? What will I consider a success by then?

Co-coaching

Choose a member of another family and share your development plan with him or her. Arrange two follow-up meetings after two months and after six months to see how well you have implemented your plan.

CLASSROOM LEARNING

Case discussion

Read company history 1 and discuss the following questions:

How did the family structure prepare and initiate the process of business transformation and generational change?

What was the role of inclusiveness, i.e. the involvement of all family members, in the process?

Read company history 2 and discuss the following questions:

How did the family use an age-related leadership transition to reinvigorate a much-needed business transformation?

What role did communication play in maintaining the momentum of this business transformation?

Read company history 3 and discuss the following questions:

How did the family use the IPO to transform the business and transition at the same time?

What can we learn from this case about successfully embedding transformation in a family business?

Read company history 4 and discuss the following questions:

How did the father and son manage to find different yet complementary paths in the transition to corporate management?

How did they mark the various milestones in the transformation process, including the final phase?

Oxford-style debate

Form two teams and prepare to debate the following thesis, with one team in favour and the other team against:

> A successful transformation in the family business follows the same rules as a transformation in a large publicly listed corporation.

Conduct a debate to collect all possible and valid arguments for and against the proposal.

Case report

Choose a family business that you know or are familiar with and analyse how they successfully managed a strategy, governance or sustainability transformation. Make concrete suggestions on how to further improve the transformation.

12 Learning opportunities

Understand, discuss, apply and share

Every family business faces its own context and goes its own way. This book describes what can be done and what has been done, rather than what should be done, and is intended as a resource for family businesses. We aim to help readers find what they need, develop techniques to talk about it and share what works for them with a broader community. Intended for anyone connected to a family business – members of the family, non-family executives and board members, external advisers – this book breaks new ground in the study of family business by showing how to bridge the gap between the generations. To do so in a manner that speaks to multiple audiences and different generations, we draw upon original company histories, suggestive fictional cases and multidisciplinary conceptual analyses. Our aim is to motivate readers to reflect upon their own circumstances, discuss the issues they identify with members of the family and interact with the wider family business community. As such, this book is intended as an invitation to learn about a new way of doing things in an age-old setting. Family businesses have existed for as long as we can trace the history of business. Indeed, some of them are many centuries old.[1] The challenge, as it were, is to teach an old dog new tricks.

This book presents a new mindset in family business. A different way of thinking implies a transition, in this case a transition from hierarchical succession to collegial co-evolution. In the first nine chapters of the book, trust maturity, capability appreciation and role respect are described as critical enablers for the Current and Next Gens to evolve as equals. Chapter 10 describes the leadership practices that some family businesses have adopted to support the transition. Chapter 11 provides insights on how to develop and run transformation initiatives that support the transition. As we have noted elsewhere, it is difficult to speak of specific stages in this very fluid transition process and different families are at different points. The transition from hierarchical to peer-based leadership is by definition a learning journey with many twists and turns, rather than a clear, precisely definable project. How do individuals and their families get started on this journey? What kind of learning works best in what situation? And, most importantly, how can all those connected in some way to family business and reading this book to help them make sense out of what they are experiencing, get the most out of the learning process?

Self-learning, moderated workshop learning and classroom learning: Different contexts for different purposes

In the recommended use of this book, we need to differentiate between three different learning contexts: self-learning for the individual reader working alone; moderated workshop learning in a family or group of families setting; and classroom learning in an executive education programme geared towards family business. All three contexts can be suitable for family business practitioners, as well as students of family business, depending on the learning style they prefer to adopt and on the circumstances in which the learning takes place. The three approaches can also be combined well, as they complement each other. In the following, we describe the three learning contexts separately, and then show how they work together.

Self-learning

The focal student for self-learning with this book is a member of a business family who wants to work on and improve collaboration between the generations in his/her own personal context. In other words, our advice for self-learning is primarily aimed at Current Gens and Next Gens who aim to make use of the side-by-side approach in a way that suits their own family and their own business. In this setting, self-learning involves taking a long, hard look at the family business in the light of the questions raised in the book, and exploring how and where the material we have presented can be applied. It is a matter of matching needs with concepts and thinking about what might work. As such, both Current Gen and Next Gen can engage in self-learning. Generally, self-learning involves both self-assessment and self-reflection (see below for definitions and examples from the book), assessing where the individual and the family stand relative to the benchmarks set out in the book and reflecting upon what to do about any gaps in performance. A concrete development plan followed by an action review may also come out of the self-learning process. Self-learning can be an end in itself, but, in many cases, self-learning leads family business readers to want to share thoughts and insights with others from the family, and with other family businesses going through similar experiences. Indeed, self-learning is often the start of something bigger, as the following examples demonstrate.

In numerous cases we have come across, self-learning starts from an interest in finding out about best practice. Whether inspired by reading about other family businesses in the press or by talking about other family businesses with friends and trusted colleagues, the individual member of a business family begins to think about his/her family business in comparison with others and decides to educate himself/herself. More often than not, the individual is actually surprised to find out that a significant body of research about family business exists and that family businesses around the world share a number of fundamental traits. The recognition that one is not alone is comforting and revealing, opening the door to a whole set of possible paths of action. In a smaller number of cases, self-learning arises out of a specific problem setting. Thus, pressing questions about topics such as career choice, internal rivalry or indeed leadership succession can prompt the individual member of a business family to seek help from texts such as this one. Self-assessment and self-reflection in the light of the reading, in turn, often motivates the individual to take the next step and involve other members of the family and/or friends from other family businesses.

In the case of one of the family businesses we have worked with, self-learning based on the recommendation of a close associate motivated the brother-in-law and business partner of the family principal to contact us and set out on a journey of moderated workshop learning with multiple workshops involving many members of the family and several generations, and eventually leading to the development and approval of a new family business governance document. In another case we are familiar with, reading and personal study led a young member of the Next Gen of one family business to found a regional working group of Next Gens dedicated to learning from each other and from external facilitators, and organize a series of distinctive moderated workshop learning experiences. In other words, self-learning often, if not always, can be the starting point for something bigger, involving several members of the family and/or multiple families in working groups designed to share experiences and, in some instances, drive change in the participating family business(es).

Moderated workshop learning

Moderated workshop learning takes place in groups consisting of several family members or representatives of multiple families and necessarily involves the presence of a moderator or facilitator. The moderator may be an educator or a consultant and the moderator's brief can range from purely educational to educational and advisory, depending on the topic chosen and the needs of the family or families taking part. In fact, a moderated workshop may be a very good way to kick off consulting work for a family business, because it can serve to bring all of the relevant stakeholders together and align them around a broader objective. As opposed to self-learning, which is primarily introspective, moderated workshop learning centres on sharing experiences in a group. As such, moderated workshop learning includes techniques like group discussion around a specific topic, case discussion in the light of a real-world case presented by the moderator and/or cases from the participants, and case simulation with role-play that allows the participants to experience the challenges of a particular case from the points of view of different protagonists. As with self-learning, a development plan and an action review may be among the desired outcomes of a moderated workshop learning process. In contrast to self-learning, however, moderated workshop learning exploits the potential for co-coaching that exists in a group of diverse individuals that have come together to work on the same questions, both within families and across families, with the support of the moderator.

There is no one typical moderated workshop learning experience. The process and the outcome depend on the specific topic, the particular mix of participants and the scope and skill of the moderator. Indeed, one moderated workshop learning experience can lead to another. Thus, in one moderated workshop learning situation we were involved in, what started out as a family day devoted to the discussion of generic family issues such as communication, information sharing and joint activity, led to an agreement for a series of further moderated workshop learning sessions focused on the establishment of a family council. In other words, moderated workshop learning experiences often stand at the beginning of a longer process that brings about concrete changes in the family business. The quality of being relatively open-ended makes moderated workshop learning exciting – for the participants and for the moderator. Questions lead to further questions, and there is no telling in advance exactly where the process may wind up. What makes a moderated workshop learning process take off is the ability to let others in on your concerns and build on shared experiences. In more ways than one, moderated workshop learning is a team-building exercise. In the special case of different family businesses coming together to learn from each other, moderated workshop learning can provide an excellent launch pad for team-building both within families and across families.

Classroom learning

When we speak of classroom learning, we are referring to the learning that takes place in executive education and masters courses dedicated to exploring strategy, governance and transformation in family businesses. What distinguishes classroom learning from moderated workshop learning is the breadth of topics covered and the range of participants. In general, classroom learning will be further removed from the concrete concerns of the individual family business and will also involve participants with a less immediate connection to family business issues. Thus, there will not be as much space to discuss specific situations, but more time allotted to working through broader, more abstract questions about the nature of family business. Group discussion of such questions, as well as discussion and role-play based on a specific case, are integral and time-tested elements of classroom learning in business education. In addition, instructors using this book may find it useful to work with Oxford-style debates to sharpen participants' arguments and participant-prepared case reports about family businesses that they are familiar with to apply classroom learning. The challenge in classroom learning is to keep the material relevant for both those participants intimately involved in family businesses (i.e. members of family businesses attending a course) and those participants with a more detached, academic interest in the subject.

Classroom learning and self-learning reinforce each other. In not a few cases, family members taking part in executive courses on family business will build on the opportunity for self-reflection offered by the course to think about and also write about the issues faced by their own family business. Thus, classroom learning can be the starting point for both self-learning and, eventually, moderated workshop learning, as the family member participating in the course is motivated by the questions raised in class to take a deeper look and revisit some of the certainties that he/she has come to accept in thinking about how the family business works and governs itself. In fact, we are aware of cases in which family members who had given up on thinking about issues like succession or governance in their own family business took learning from class as an instigator for taking up the issues again and doing something about them. In a reciprocal manner, self-learning can lead to classroom learning, as members of family businesses who have started the processes of self-assessment and self-reflection on their own seek a formalized framework for continuing their education. Not a few Next Gens we have encountered in our business school classes are there precisely because they want to gain the conceptual background that will enable them to confidently address the present and future needs of their family businesses.

Self-learning, moderated workshop learning, classroom learning: A virtuous circle?

Self-learning, moderated workshop learning and classroom learning are complementary and reinforce each other. In the ideal case, as outlined in the examples above, one form of learning leads to another, and it doesn't matter from where in the circle the learning begins (see Figure 12.1).

As with any kind of learning, individual curiosity and willingness to explore new ideas is essential to initiating learning in the family business setting. Over and above individual proclivities, we find that the influence of peers, from both within and outside the family business, plays an important role in encouraging the learning process. It helps a lot to have someone positively disposed and genuinely interested to talk to, even if the learning journey starts out as a purely personal project for the individual family member (self-learning, classroom learning). Sometimes, self-learning motivates individuals to look for new peers in other family businesses with the help of the various networks that connect families and especially Next Gens; in other cases, classroom learning experiences lead directly to new friendships that allow individuals from different families to bond over shared questions.

Figure 12.1 Learning in a virtuous circle

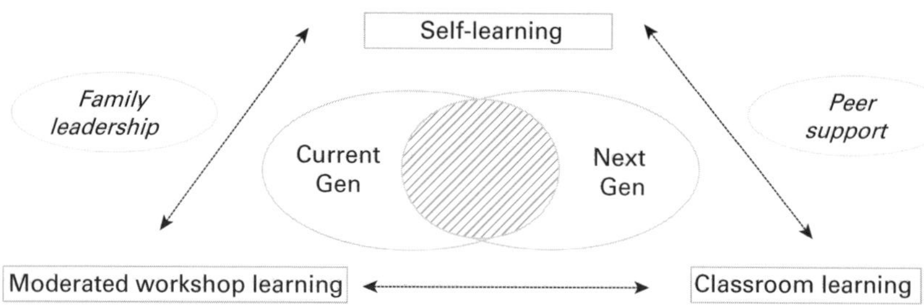

Moderated workshop learning, in turn, is based on the principle of building on shared experiences among peers. For moderated workshop learning to really take off and enable change, however, supportive peer groups are not enough. What is required is leadership – not so much from the facilitator, but from among the family member participants. A person willing to lead can motivate others to engage in self-learning and ensure that what is discussed in the workshop receives adequate follow-up. The absence of process leadership makes it much more difficult, if not impossible, to turn moderated workshop learning into tangible change efforts. Last but not least, all three learning contexts depend upon the participants' willingness to temporarily put day-to-day business concerns aside and actually focus on learning. As long as day-to-day activities dominate, it is very hard to open minds to learning, no matter how supportive the learning context.

This book is designed to support each of the three learning contexts, as indicated in the learning journey section at the end of each chapter. We have organized the learning journey into pit stops to help readers to better understand, discuss and apply what they have read, and then share their experience and expertise with each other. Ten pedagogical tools are used to help readers navigate their personal learning journeys.

Ten pedagogical tools for the learning journey: Definition and examples of use

Understand (self-learning)

1. Self-assessment

Self-assessment involves individual family members reflecting on their own or their organization's abilities, strengths, weaknesses and overall performance.[2]

> **TIP**
>
> Example from Chapter 1:
>
> *Assess where the Current Gen and the Next Gen in your family business are and should be on the continuum between parent/child and adult conversations.*

The idea of this exercise of self-assessment is for both Current Gen and Next Gen readers to benchmark their own experience with intergenerational conversations against the standard of adult conversations described in Chapter 1. In this way, and if they have not already started thinking about it like this, family business readers can make the material presented in the book more personally relevant to them. By definition, the self-assessment will not be a precise benchmarking exercise, but only provides a rough estimate. In fact, the self-assessment serves as an easy, straightforward way of relating to the material and kicking off the process of self-reflection. If the self-assessment indicates room for improvement, then the reader is motivated to go deeper and continue the self-learning to explore why and in what way his/her own conversations are not up to standard.

2. Self-reflection

Self-reflection allows individual family members to examine their thoughts, emotions and actions with a view to questioning assumptions and long-held beliefs.

TIP

Example from Chapter 1:

Current Gen: Think through the following statements. How true are they of your own situation?

I know how to talk with members of the Next Gen: I understand them.

When I talk with the Next Gen, it's from one adult to another.

I keep parent/child patterns out of conversations with the Next Gen.

Next Gen: Think through the following statements – how true are they of your own situation?

I know how to talk with members of the Current Gen: I understand them.

When I talk with the Current Gen, it's from one adult to another.

I keep parent/child patterns out of conversations with the Current Gen.

The self-reflection exercise picks up where the self-assessment leaves off and provides specific questions for readers to compare their experience against and think through. In particular, it asks Current Gens and Next Gens to consider whether their conversations with each other are really going the way they think they are, and the way they would like. The obvious corollary of these questions is, 'If not, then why not?' The self-reflection may or may not lead to discussion in the family, but it represents an important first step in helping both Current Gens and Next Gens to face the issues raised in Chapter 1. In the ideal case, self-learning kicks off a learning journey that leads from recognition to action. In other words, self-reflection is often the starting point for an individual family member to think about organizing a moderated workshop for the family or signing up for a classroom learning experience.

Discuss (moderated workshop learning, classroom learning)

3. Group discussion

The group discussion serves as a forum for individuals to come together to exchange ideas, share perspectives and collectively explore a topic or problem.

TIP

Example from Chapter 1, moderated workshop learning:

Use the material presented in Chapter 1 as a launch pad for thinking about and critically discussing how the family approaches conversations.

For the Current Gen, first prepare yourself, then discuss with the Next Gen:

> When do conversations with the Next Gen about the family business (i.e. topics, settings) go especially well?
>
> When do they go poorly?

For the Next Gen, first prepare yourself, then discuss with the Current Gen:

> When do conversations with the Current Gen about the family business (i.e. topics, settings) go especially well?
>
> When do they go poorly?

TIP

Example from Chapter 1, classroom learning:

Use the material presented in Chapter 1 as a launch pad for thinking about and critically discussing how families approach conversations.

When do conversations between the Current and Next Gen about the family business go especially well?

When do they go poorly?

For moderated workshop learning, the group discussion is focused on the experience of the family or families present; for classroom learning, the group discussion is necessarily more general, asking participants to reflect on their knowledge of intergenerational conversations in family businesses from all possible sources. The objectives of the group discussion in both cases are similar: to surface examples of and think about what makes these conversations go well or poorly. In a moderated workshop, the discussion is likely to be immediate and personal to the family, and it can be a challenge to integrate conceptual learning from Chapter 1; in a classroom, on the other hand, the discussion may stay abstract, limited to conceptual observations. In either situation, the challenge is to avoid the extremes and make sure that the discussion stays focused and relevant.

4. Case discussion

The case discussion follows a pedagogical approach that combines theoretical knowledge with real-world problem-solving on the basis of an event or a history.

TIP

Example from Chapter 1:

Read fictional case 1 and discuss the following questions:

Put yourself in the position of Grace: how should Grace react to Henry's offer to arrange an internship at LVMH?

Put yourself in the position of Henry: how should Henry react to the business plan Grace will present to him?

As a consultant to the family, how would you advise Grace and Henry to raise the level of their communications?

In a moderated workshop setting, participating families and family members can have a tendency to see aspects of themselves in the case and may want to focus discussion on these right away. For the quality of the learning experience, it is advisable to stick to the facts of the case as they are presented, at least in the first stages of the workshop. Doing so will allow the participants to go beyond the limitations of their personal experience and open their minds to the broader issues affecting intergenerational conversations in family businesses. In the classroom setting, these broader issues will emerge more readily. In both settings, the objective of the case discussion is to permit participants to recognize the salience of the issues and think through the range of possible solutions as an outside observer. In a second stage, the issues raised in the case study can be revisited in the light of the participant family's (or families') experiences, as a key to sharing their own experiences with each other and unlocking their own questions.

5. Case simulation

The case simulation is an immersive learning method that replicates real-world scenarios and usually involves role-play.

TIP

Example from Chapter 1:

Replay the conversation between Grace and her father in your own words.

For the Next Gen, assume the role of Grace's father.

For the Current Gen, assume the role of Grace.

Starting positions: Grace reacts to Henry's offer of an LVMH internship; Henry reacts to Grace's business plan.

Those who are not involved in the simulation observe and comment.

The case simulation can be used as a follow-up to the case discussion or as a stand-alone exercise. Whereas the case discussion centres around arguing the merits of different positions, the case simulation focuses attention on the roles played by the different generations. As such, the case simulation offers participants an opportunity to try out a variety of approaches to bridging the conversation gap that separates the Current Gen and the Next Gen in the fictional case study. Compared to trying out different conversation approaches on issues of actual concern to the family business(es) taking part in a moderated workshop, the case simulation has the great advantage of lowered risk. What is tried out in the case simulation, especially following the instructions for the Current Gen and the Next Gen to reverse roles, may provide more than merely food for thought and indicate a new way forward. Less practically impactful, but no less dramatic in a classroom setting, the role-play around which the case simulation revolves will serve to make concepts tangible and surface emotions.

6. Oxford-style debate

The Oxford-style debate is a structured and formalized method of argumentation that traces its origins to the debating traditions of the Oxford Union.[3]

TIP

Example from Chapter 1:

Form two teams and prepare to debate the following thesis, with one team in favour and the other team against:

> It is the job of the Current Gen to create the conditions that allow for a peer-to-peer conversation between the Current Gen and the Next Gen.

Conduct a debate to collect all possible and valid arguments for and against the proposal.

While it can be used for a moderated workshop, the Oxford-style debate is primarily intended for a classroom setting in which the participants do not have a strong personal connection to the material (i.e. where the majority of participants do not have a family business background). The Oxford-style debate starts at a more abstract level than the case discussion and may be used as a complement or as an alternative to mix up the classroom experience. The key to making the Oxford-style debate work in the classroom is to create a sense of competition among participants (while strictly following the time-honoured rules established for this type of debate). To ensure this happens, it is important that the class leader (instructor) emphasizes the contrast between the opposing positions and encourages participants to take ownership of 'their' side.

Apply (self-learning, moderated workshop learning)

7. Development plan for Current Gen/Next Gen

The development plan is a strategic road map designed to guide an individual or an organization toward achieving specific goals.

> **TIP**
>
> Example from Chapter 1:
>
> *Draw up a development plan in which you define the following milestones:*
>
> Short term: What will I do by next week to close the conversation gap? What will I consider a success by then?
>
> Medium term: What will I do by next month to close the conversation gap? What will I consider a success by then?
>
> Long term: What will I do by next year to close the conversation gap? What will I consider a success by then?

The development plan can emerge from self-learning or moderated workshop learning. In the former case, the individual learner creates a personal development plan on the basis of self-assessment and self-reflection. In the latter case, it is the group or team of participants (i.e. the members of a family taking part in a workshop) who agree on the development plan, based on what they take away from the workshop and the specific action steps they have decided to implement. Either way, the identification of a specific gap that needs to be closed is central to the development plan. The better specified and the more tangible the gap, the easier it will be for the participant(s) to define achievement levels and track their progress over time. As for many other change actions described in this book, it may be better to start with something relatively small and doable, rather than wanting to make drastic moves and becoming discouraged in the face of lack of motivation or resistance. In any case, the development plan goes hand in hand with the action review (see below).

8. Action review

The action review is a structured and reflective process designed to evaluate achievement of a development plan and learn from past experience.

> **TIP**
>
> Example from Chapter 1:
>
> *Mark the dates in your calendar when you check how well you have achieved the short-, medium- and long-term goals you set. Evaluate what you have achieved and look back at what went well and what went poorly.*

The action review is a means to impose discipline on participants as well as a means for self-learners and participants to impose discipline on themselves. The development plan described above only represents a starting point for action. Without a detailed and credible action review, with monthly or, at a minimum, quarterly assessment points, even the most well-defined development plan is likely to remain unfulfilled. However, the robust action review does more than just measure achievements against goals. Just as important as measurement of progress in bridging a perceived performance gap is analysis of personal growth. In effect, the timely action review provides space for periodically thinking about and evaluating why and how progress has occurred (or failed to occur) and reflecting on what additional steps might need to be taken. In other words, the action review functions as a living document.

Share (moderated workshop learning, classroom learning)

9. Co-coaching

Co-coaching is a collaborative and reciprocal approach to professional development where individuals actively engage in coaching each other.

> **TIP**
>
> Example from Chapter 1:
>
> *Choose a partner from a different generation and share your development plan with him or her. Arrange two follow-up meetings after two months and after six months to see how well you have implemented your plan.*

Co-coaching works well in a moderated workshop learning setting and represents a very useful complement to the development plan. Essentially, the co-coaching tool revolves around the dynamic that is established between two individuals in the workshop, ideally from different families and different backgrounds (i.e. different generations, as specified in the instructions above, or professional experiences, or cultural heritages). The two individuals can keep each other accountable, checking on each other's progress and offering encouragement. Even more importantly, the two individuals – *because* they have different points of view – can continue to offer intellectual stimulation to each other, long after the workshop itself is completed. Coming from different families, the co-coaching partners will be able to serve as independent sounding boards, without the emotional baggage that can get in the way of individuals from the same family. In the best of cases, co-coaching leads to lasting relationships between individuals and between families.

10. Case report

The case report is a detailed and comprehensive document that provides an in-depth description and analysis of a particular case, based on substantial research.

> **TIP**
>
> Example from Chapter 1:
>
> *Choose a family business that you know or are familiar with, and analyse how the conversations between the Current and Next Gen are going and how they have evolved over time. Make concrete suggestions on how the conversations could be further improved to make them truly peer-to-peer.*

The case report is used in the classroom setting to give non-family business participants an opportunity to examine the ideas presented in the book in the light of the real-world experience of a family business that they choose to study. Preparing the case report involves considerable primary and secondary research. The usefulness of the case report as a learning tool depends on the level of familiarity that participants already have or can establish with a family business in their personal contexts. Absent such familiarity, it will not be possible for participants to gain enough insight into how a family business works to make for a useful case report. If, on the other hand, participants do get the chance to work closely with a family business for the purposes of the case report, their learning from the report may in turn also serve the family that has agreed to be the focus of study.

Mapping the learning journey

For the sake of immediacy, we address the following practical recommendations concerning the learning journey directly to the family business reader. Once you know where you want to go (as described in Chapters 1 to 10), how to get there (Chapter 11) and what tools are available to you (Chapter 12, to this point), it is time to put the pieces together and develop maps to show you the way. Let's take a look at a set of maps that can help on your learning journey, for yourself and for your family, building on the ten learning tools presented above.

Setting priorities for your learning journey

Based on your own and the other family members' self-reflection and self-assessment, you will have developed a thorough understanding of where you are and where you want to go. Even if each individual family member has a good understanding of their personal point of view, how can the different perspectives be brought together? The gap profiler (Figure 12.2) not only helps to identify the gap between the perceived current state and the desired target state along the nine enabling dimensions presented in this book, but also can serve to display different points of view in the family.

Visualizing the different assessment curves provides a good basis for identifying where everyone stands, but also where the biggest gaps are and therefore where the priorities of the journey should lie. This can be achieved

Figure 12.2 Gap profiler

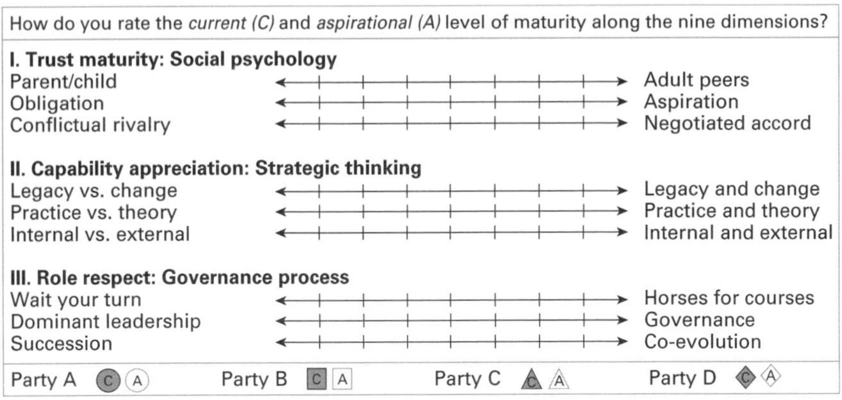

in three steps. First, each family member shows their curve and explains the reasons for their rating. In a second step, all participants identify the dimensions where there is consensus and those where the assessments differ significantly. The latter are then discussed in more detail in a third step with the goal of reaching a consensus on which dimensions should be prioritized.

Charting your learning journey

Once a consensus has been reached on the current and desired state of the family business, the transition must be planned in detail. This also requires anticipating possible tailwinds and headwinds along the way. What external conditions can facilitate the transition and thus create opportunities, and what factors can bring additional challenges along the way? Discussing these opportunities and challenges has a dual purpose. First, it puts everyone involved and affected in the right, or rather realistic, frame of mind. Second, it provides the basis for defining the various steps required to achieve the desired state.

The steps must be detailed enough to be allocated adequate resources, and comprehensive enough to cover all the activities required to get from the current to the aspirational state. In this sense, the aspiration map (Figure 12.3) helps to visualize the results of the self-assessment, group discussion and co-coaching. Using a visualization for this step has two key advantages. First, it helps to identify any gaps in planning. Second, it serves as a valuable communication tool that can also be used to show all family members involved how the transition is unfolding.

Figure 12.3 Aspiration map

Timing your learning journey

A thorough definition of the steps is a useful first stage in charting your learning journey, but it only gains its true value when it is complemented by appointing an owner and allocating a timeline. Ultimately, the journey needs to be viewed as a project, or rather a series of projects, with fixed start and end dates. Looking at the journey in this way has several advantages. First, it leads to realistic expectations among all those involved as to what can be achieved by when. Second, it allows the critical paths to be identified so that potential risks become visible. Third, such a plan with clear timelines and accountability provides the basis for monitoring progress. The transition road map (Figure 12.4) builds on the development plan and serves as the basis for the action review.

Figure 12.4 Transition road map

Steps	Owner	Timeline
Step 1		
Step 2		
Step 3		
Step 4		
Step 5		
Step 6		
Step 7		
Step 8		
Step 9		
Step 10		

Debating your learning journey

While the first three maps (Figures 12.2, 12.3 and 12.4) are central to planning and monitoring the entire learning journey, the following two maps help to fine-tune the process by incorporating the knowledge gained along the way and adjusting the course if necessary.

As described in the previous chapters, there will be many debates during the journey about which direction to take, given the different interests and perspectives of family members. In such situations, it is valuable to have a map at hand that outlines a process for dealing with such differences. As we have seen in Chapter 3, addressing disagreement is all about fair process, i.e. how the issues are resolved rather than a particular outcome.

The debate navigator (Figure 12.5) provides a framework for reaching a consensus. It is based on the idea that a repeated exchange of arguments that

Figure 12.5 Debate navigator

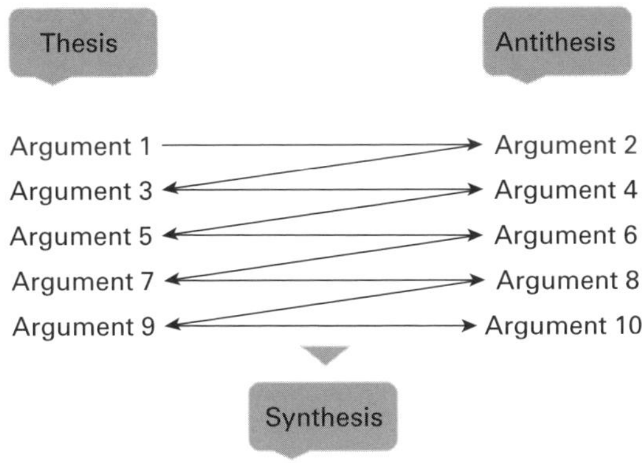

support a thesis and an antithesis will ultimately lead to a synthesis if all the different facets of a topic are considered. It goes back to the German philosopher Johann Fichte (1762–1814), who formulated the triad of thesis, antithesis and synthesis as an approach to solving important philosophical puzzles. This approach has another advantage: it ensures that every argument is taken into account and that all parties involved are heard (i.e. fair process).

Reflecting on your learning journey

No matter how well the journey is planned and how smooth the course that is followed, there will still be surprises. At best, these surprises will lead to new insights that can be put into practice. Surprising insights may come from self-reflection, case discussion, case simulation, or co-coaching, but also from other real discoveries along the way.

The journey logbook (Figure 12.6) is intended as a repository for such discoveries, a kind of diary for the family. It allows you to list every significant event, derive insights from it and reflect on the implications for the journey. A logbook not only serves as a reflection at the moment of the event, but also provides a valuable record of events in retrospect. If everyone involved agrees, various logbooks can even be used to analyse and evaluate the progress of family-wide learning efforts. This can provide valuable insights into the dynamics of the transition and indicate what can be improved to make the journey even more meaningful and effective.

Figure 12.6 Journey logbook

Date	Event	Insight	Implications

KEY TAKEAWAYS

1. Self-learning, moderated workshop learning and classroom learning go together.
2. Family business learning requires someone to take responsibility for the process.
3. Families have different objectives; their learning journeys will be different.

EPILOGUE

In the book's introduction we wrote the following about generational transition in the family business: 'More often than not, the hierarchical nature of the parent/child relationship gets in the way of effective collaboration. A new mindset is needed.' Over the course of the three years we have spent researching and writing this book, talking and working with many families around the world, our conviction about the need for a fresh approach to age-old questions has only become stronger. To be absolutely clear, we do not think hierarchy in the family business is dead. On the contrary, hierarchy is alive and well: time and again, we see hierarchical gulfs like parent/child, senior/junior or experience/fresh take get in the way of effective collaboration between the generations. Instead of wishing away hierarchy, we offer a framework for addressing it in all of its facets. With the material presented over the preceding twelve chapters, business families and their advisers can put together and implement their own transition plan, depending on the specifics of the family and the business. The idea is not to throw everything we know about family business overboard, but rather to develop an approach that takes both old certainties and new realities into account. As outlined in Chapter 10, the challenge is to find ways to attune the collective constraints required for organizational continuity with the individual aspirations critical to personal growth. We sincerely hope that the company histories, fictional case studies and multidisciplinary conceptual analyses we have presented help families bridge the gap between the generations.

Trying something new is always a leap of faith. Take the effort made by several families in our study to 'defy age preconceptions' (see Chapter 10). Hierarchy puts established position over potential contribution. By defying age preconceptions and counting on the potential contribution of the Next Gen rather than insisting on established position as the measure of worth, these families are incurring novel risks, namely the risks of overwhelming the Next Gen and unsettling the Current Gen and, in the process, damaging the business. It would seemingly be easier to have the Next Gen repeat the Current Gen's own well-worn path of slow apprenticeship. *Plus ça change, plus c'est la même chose*. Would the easier way also be the better way, or even the safer way? Throughout this book, we have argued that productive years of collaborative overlap between a Current Gen still in complete command of its entrepreneurial powers and a Next Gen ready to take on the world present a unique opportunity for family businesses to adapt to rapidly changing markets and to stay relevant. In our view, the model of slow apprenticeship bears the greater risks: failure of the business to adapt fast enough and, just as dangerous for the family and the business, failure to engage the Next Gen.

The core concepts introduced in this book – trust maturity, capability appreciation and role respect – enable the generations to productively co-evolve as peers. The leadership practices we have described, in turn, the very leadership practices that many of the families we have studied employ to navigate the transition towards new ways of creating value together, provide a baseline for implementing a gradual and effective succession. The book provides extensive material for self-learning, moderated workshop learning and classroom learning, all geared towards improving understanding between the generations and enhancing collaboration. Our approach emphasizes the recognition of individual differences in people and stresses the importance of inclusion based on the value of diverse contributions: within the framework provided, each Current Gen and each Next Gen can find their own place. Following the side-by-side approach may even motivate erstwhile non-contributors who have chosen to stay outside the business to contribute in their own way, i.e. on the ownership committee, on the family council, or, one step further removed, with the family foundation. Where there is genuine role respect between the generations, working in the business does not have to be a prerequisite or necessary condition for taking part in shaping the future of the family business. People do change and relationships evolve: neither the Current Gen nor the Next Gen stands still. Thus, our conclusion in Chapter 1 was: not to get stuck in positions or roles and not to think you 'know each other' once and for all. Indeed, not acknowledging the possibility of personal development on *both* sides of the generation gap is a big barrier to cultivating trust maturity, capability appreciation and role respect. A side-by-side mindset increases the probability of positive surprises, for the family and for the business.

Broader implications: Within the family business and beyond

The focus of this book has been on the relationship between the Current Gen and the Next Gen of family business leaders, the members of the family who own the business. Nevertheless, the mindset shift we have described also has significant implications for non-family stakeholders in the business, especially senior non-family employees and non-family board members. We have already pointed out that these senior individuals can and often do play important roles in the development of the Next Gen. The key take-away for them from our analysis is to recognize and support the side-by-side mindset. In their interactions with members of the Next Gen, this means focusing on integrating them in decision-making, rather than isolating them and hoping they will go away; and challenging them, rather than coddling them and assuming they don't really want to put in the hard work or the time. In their interactions with the Current Gen, senior non-family employees and non-family board members are called upon more than ever to serve as candid sparring partners and to help build bridges between the generations. If fully trusted by both the Current Gen and the Next Gen, senior non-family can be the linchpin for taking the family business to the next level of collaboration.

Today's Next Gen, over and above the classical impatience of youth, is characterized by big-picture thinking. As we have seen, firm-level questions of strategy, sustainability and governance concern the Next Gen just as much as, if not more than, learning on the job and personal career advancement. Not only that, they have grown up with evidence of very rapid change everywhere, with many of the most striking advances driven by young entrepreneurs and achieved over a short time span. The Next Gen insists on a place at the big table, where the future of the family and the business is being discussed. In the ideal case, and if supported by the Current Gen, big-picture thinking and entrepreneurial impatience in the Next Gen lead to the kind of successful strategy, sustainability and governance transformation initiatives we have reported in this book. More often than not, change in the family business comes from within, driven by both generations' sense of purpose and long-term orientation. We definitely think family businesses are capable of transforming themselves on their own.

What do our findings about intergenerational collaboration and transformation drive mean for advisers to the family business, namely, consultants, lawyers and bankers? For advisers of all stripes, the key question is, who is the client? Advisers' narrow focus on the Current Gen as client may mask the rise of the Next Gen and prevent them from appropriately adapting their services. Not that advisers do not already consider the Next Gen; they do and there is a plethora of enticing propositions, mostly free of charge, for members of the Next Gen to choose from. What our analysis suggests is that advisers to family business may want to recalibrate their offer, away from getting access to the Next Gen as future clients and towards working with them and the Current Gen as partners for the long haul. Increasingly, the

Current Gen and the Next Gen are coming to the table together; the client is not one, but several. When the different generations do come to the table together, advisers may find a new role for themselves in supporting transformation initiatives, helping the family business bridge the gaps between legacy and change, practice and theory, and internal and external knowledge. To do so effectively, advisers to family businesses will need to venture beyond their own specialist boundaries, engaging with each other to provide whatever customized, multidisciplinary service the transformation requires.

One of the most striking characteristics of the Next Gen of family business leaders is their concern, already at a relatively young age, for the health and future viability of the enterprise, as a whole (see also Chapters 5 and 7). This broad concern for the whole clearly distinguishes the Next Gen at a family business from their non-family business peers, who, as regular employees, will not feel the same far-reaching sense of responsibility. Nonetheless, younger people at non-family firms, too, have grown up with rapid change all around them and business schools have also prepared them to engage in big-picture thinking. Quite naturally, therefore, we are led to ask whether and to what extent the side-by-side approach could be applied outside the context of the family business. More particularly, how might C-suite executives at non-family firms benefit from building closer, peer-to-peer ties with younger leaders inside the organization? Programmes at a few larger companies that provide for young hires to reverse-mentor senior executives offer evidence that this kind of thinking is making inroads.[1] However, at least at the senior level, these are still few and far between. In a sense, then, the competitive necessity of involving the Next Gen in big-picture decisions and integrating them in transformation initiatives gives family businesses another source of potential advantage over their non-family counterparts.

Whether the individual family business takes up the side-by-side challenge or persists with a traditional, hierarchical approach to intergenerational collaboration is an important choice, but it is not all-or-nothing. Transformation initiatives that require young and old to work together provide a very good platform for overcoming hierarchical barriers between the generations. As we have seen, such initiatives are also good for business. Each family business has a unique starting point and each family business has its own capacity for change. This book makes the case for adopting a new mindset and provides the concepts and tools required to make peer-based collaboration across generations in family business a reality. We look forward to working with families across various learning contexts to help them make the transition.

NOTES

Introduction

1 We follow Miller et al in defining family firms as 'those in which multiple members of the same family are involved as major owners or managers, either contemporaneously or over time'. D Miller, I Le-Breton Miller, R H Lester and A A Canella. Are family firms really superior performers? *Journal of Corporate Finance*, 2007, 13 (5), 836.

2 The next generation of family business leaders includes individuals aged 20 plus to 40 plus, who are: a) at university; b) in a full-time job at the family business; c) in a full-time job outside the family business; or d) considering coming (back) to the family business mid-career.

3 For a discussion of the meaning of sustainability in the family business context and a review of the associated literature, see J J Ferreira, C I Fernandes, F Schiavone and R V Mahto. Sustainability in family business: A bibliometric study and research agenda, *Technological Forecasting and Social Change*, 2021, 173.

4 It is worth noting that a number of family businesses are already leaders in their industries when it comes to questions of environmental and social sustainability. Our concern is with intergenerational collaboration on sustainability issues.

5 Our particular focus is on how the generations can learn to work together in the family business; for a general sociological treatment of intergenerational exchange in families, see M Szydlik (2017) *Sharing Lives: Adult children and parents*, Routledge, Abingdon.

6 In many family businesses, particularly larger ones with multiple layers of organization, the relationships between Current Gen and Next Gen are to some degree moderated by senior non-family members. For example, senior non-family may function as colleagues of the Next Gen on transformation initiatives; as direct superiors of the Next Gen in operational roles; and as trusted sounding boards for the Current Gen on issues ranging from strategy to succession. Indeed, in some family businesses, non-family are explicitly tasked with mentoring and rendering objective judgement on the progress of the Next Gen.

7 Although not completely independent, trust maturity, capability appreciation and role respect are conceptually distinct and therefore require separate treatment.

8 Our focus on interpersonal relationships between the generations finds echoes in a noteworthy study of next generation leaders: K Kandade, G Samara, M J Parada and A Dawson. From family successors to successful business leaders: A qualitative study of how high-quality relationships develop in family businesses, *Journal of Family Business Strategy*, 2021, 12 (2). As do we, Kandade et al emphasize the importance of trust and respect.

9 For a relevant and historically insightful treatment of inheritance laws, see L M Friedman (2009) *Dead Hands: A social history of wills, trust and inheritance law*, Stanford University Press, Stanford, CA.

10 In Chapter 2 we will demonstrate that aspiration rather than obligation forms one of the critical bases for peer-based collaboration across generations in family business. Putting aspiration over obligation also implies that those members of the next generation who do *not* want to work in the family business are not pushed to do so against their will, but rather encouraged to find careers outside. By no means do we wish to suggest that every member of the next generation should (want to) play a role in the family business.

11 It is worth noting that today more and more new businesses are being founded by groups of unrelated individuals, either as shareholdings or as partnerships (cf A C Klotz, K M Hmieleski, B H Bradley and L W Busenitz. New venture teams: A review of the literature and road map for future research, *Journal of Management*, 2014, 40). Although these businesses are not predestined to become family businesses, but rather to be grown and sold within the lifetime of the founders, some of them will go through a process of consolidation of ownership and wind up in family hands.

Part One Trust maturity: Social psychology

1 'Father and son' (1970, *Tea for the Tillerman*, Cat Music Limited).

2 For a comprehensive treatment in this vein, see K E Gersick, J A Davis, M M Hampton and I Lansberg (1997) *Generation to Generation: Life cycles of the family business*, Harvard Business School Press, Boston, MA. Another fundamental text is R A Carlock and J Ward (2001) *Strategic Planning for the Family Business: Parallel planning to unify the family and the business*, Palgrave, New York.

3 Cf J R Galbraith. Organization design: An information processing view, *Interfaces*, 1974, 4 (3), 28–36. For a more general statement of the underlying theory, see J R Galbraith (1977) *Organization Design*, Addison-Wesley, Reading, MA.

1 From parent/child to adult peers: Level conversations

1 For examples and further development of these ideas, see H James (2006) *Family Capitalism: Wendels, Haniels, Falcks and the continental European model*, Harvard University Press, Cambridge, MA.
2 Among many other contributions to knowledge about family conversations, the work of Deborah Tannen on power and solidarity (i.e. D Tannen (2001) *I Only Say This Because I Love You*, Random House, New York, drawing on R Brown and A Gilman, The pronouns of power and solidarity, in T A Sebeok (ed), *Style in Language*, MIT Press, Cambridge, MA, 253–76) and the thinking of Paul Watzlawick about homeostasis and change (i.e. P Watzlawick, J Beavin-Bavelas and D Jackson (1967) *Pragmatics of Human Communication*, Norton, New York) are especially relevant.

2 From obligation to aspiration: Reset expectations

1 I Boszormenyi-Nagy and G M Spark (1973) *Invisible Loyalties: Reciprocity in intergenerational family therapy*, Harper & Row, New York.
2 For a note on how cultures influence family values, refer to the discussion of filial piety across cultures in the Introduction.
3 For example, in 20th century Britain, as described in fascinating detail by J Finch (1991) *Family Obligations and Social Change*, Polity, Cambridge.
4 M A Klein (2018) *Trapped in the Family Business*, MK Insights LL.
5 Freedom of choice in family businesses is examined in Chapter 10, with specific examples of how to ensure that individual freedom coexists with the structures of the family business.
6 In this context, it is worth referring to Kenneth Kay's important psychological treatment of the family business as a sickness: K Kaye. When the family business is a sickness, *Family Business Review*, 1996, 9, 347–68. Kaye argues that, in some cases, particularly when the parents' ego development is inadequate, the family business functions as an addiction, for the parents because they cling to it, for the children because they are constantly anxious about it. Feelings of loyalty do not equate with addiction, but some of the symptoms of addiction that Kaye describes, namely progressive dependency and tolerance (of pain and disappointment), are also seen when loyalty holds sway over individual freedom.

3 From conflictual rivalry to negotiated accord: Apply fair process

1. See, for example, H Levinson. Conflicts that plague family businesses, *Harvard Business Review*, March 1971.
2. Refer to the Introduction for a more thorough treatment of the archetypical character of family business relationships.
3. Cf C Hartmann and S Goudarzi. Does birth order affect personality? *Scientific American*, August 2019. See also C E Watkins. Birth-order research and Adler's theory: A critical review. *Individual Psychology: Journal of Adlerian theory, research & practice*, 1992, 48, 357–68.
4. For an insightful analysis of how to comprehensively assess the relationships in the successor generation, see G Swogger, Jr. Assessing the successor generation in family business, *Family Business Review*, 1994, 4, 397–411.
5. Cf I L Janis (1972) *Victims of Groupthink*, Houghton Mifflin, Boston. To the extent that families try to avoid conflict, they can be especially prone to groupthink. See also J A Davis and R M Herrera (1998) The social psychology of family shareholder dynamics, *Family Business Review*, 11, 253–60.
6. As articulated in L Van der Heyden, C Blondel and R Carlock. Fair process: Striving for justice in family business, *Family Business Review*, 2005, 18 (1), 1–21.
7. For a thorough treatment of how family businesses can balance individual freedom and commitment to the ways of the group, see the discussion of freedom of choice in Chapter 10.
8. These restrictions may be explicit and cast in legal terms, as exemplified by trust structures that limit access to and use of funds, or implicit and merely understood, as exemplified by behavioural expectations that limit what kinds of activities are acceptable for family members to engage in.
9. H Qiu and M Freel. Managing family-related conflicts in family businesses: A review and research agenda, *Family Business Review*, 2020, 33, 90–113.

Part Two Capability appreciation: Strategic thinking

1. R G McGrath (2013) *The end of competitive advantage: How to keep your strategy moving as fast as your business*, Harvard Business Review Press, Cambridge, MA.
2. C Christensen (1997) *The Innovator's Dilemma: When new technologies cause great firms to fail*, Harvard Business Review Press, Cambridge, MA.

4 From legacy vs change to legacy *and* change: Reassess goals

1 The notion of legacy is very strong in family business, and finds broad expression in the family business literature. For thoughtful definitions, see J H Chua, J J Chrisman and P Sharma. Defining the family business by behavior, *Entrepreneurship Theory and Practice*, 1999, 23, 19–39, or D Hjorth and A Dawson. The burden of history in the family business organization, *Organization Studies*, 2016, 37, 1089–111.

2 A strand of work that is germane to our purposes focuses on determining the meaning of legacy in particular contexts, for example, L Manelli, V Magrelli, J Kotlar, A Messeni Petruzzelli and F Frattini. Building an outward-oriented social family legacy: Rhetorical history in family business foundations, *Family Business Review*, 2023, 36, 143–68.

3 R Suddaby and P Jaskiewicz. Managing traditions: A critical capability for family business success, *Family Business Review*, 2020, 33, 234–43.

4 See P Jaskiewicz, J G Combs and S B Rau. Entrepreneurial legacy: Toward a theory of how some family firms nurture transgenerational entrepreneurship, *Journal of Business Venturing*, 2015, 30, 29–49; see also H Korine (2016) *Succession For Change: Strategic transitions in family and founder-led businesses*, Palgrave Macmillan, London; or J Seaman, A Gorin and F Bernhard. How to build upon the legacy of your family business – and make it your own, *Harvard Business Review*, June 2023.

5 Cf A Calabro, M Vecciarini, J Gast, G Campopiano, A De Massis and S Kraus. Innovation in family firms: A systematic literature review and guidance for future research, *International Journal of Management Reviews*, 2019, 21.

6 W B Arthur (2009) *The Nature of Technology: What it is and how it evolves*, Free Press, New York, Introduction.

5 From practice vs theory to practice *and* theory: Review structure

1 For a very interesting psychological perspective on wisdom, see R H Trowbridge and M Ferrari. *Sophia* and *phronesis* in psychology, philosophy and traditional wisdom, *Research in Human Development*, 2011, 8, 89–94.

2 T R Schatzki, K K Cetina and E von Savigny (2001) *The Practice Turn in Contemporary Theory*, Routledge, London.

3 C Bueger and F Gadinger (2018) *International Practice Theory*, Palgrave Macmillan, London.

4 For good introductions to the ethnographic approach, see E Schein (1987) *The Clinical Perspective in Fieldwork*, Sage Publications, Newbury Park, CA, and also J Van Maanen (1988) *Tales of the Field*, University of Chicago Press, Chicago.

6 From internal vs external to internal *and* external: Rethink practices

1 H Chesbrough (2006) *Open Innovation: The new imperative for creating and profiting from technology*, Harvard Business School Press, Cambridge, MA.
2 For a recent, empirical study of the importance of secrecy in family business, see E M Gimenez-Fernandez, K Beukel, B B Tyler, N Spielmann, D Cerrato, A F Discua Cruz and M Minciullo. Should we patent it or keep it a secret? The moderating role of proactive orientation in family versus non-family SMEs, *International Small Business Journal*, 2021, 5, 450–73. For a more general discussion of secrecy and intellectual capital in family business, see K Gan, Z Saleh and M Abessi (2013) Ownership structure and voluntary disclosure of intellectual capital: Evidence from Malaysia, in N O Ndubisi (ed), *Enterprise Development in SMEs and Entrepreneurial Firms: Dynamic processes*, IGI Global, Hershey, PA, 390–404.
3 Cf J Kotlar, A De Massis, F Frattini, M Bianchi and H Fang. Technology acquisition in family and nonfamily firms: A longitudinal analysis of Spanish manufacturing firms, *Journal of Product Innovation Management*, 2013, 30.
4 R McGrath (2013) *The End of Competitive Advantage*, Harvard Business Review Press, Cambridge, MA.

Part Three Role respect: Governance processes

1 Cf G C Reese. The question of the succession in Elizabethan drama, *Studies in English*, University of Texas Press, 1942, 22, 59–85.
2 Cf H Korine (2020) *Preventing Corporate Governance Failure*, Haupt, Bern.

7 From wait your turn to horses for courses: Defy convention

1 For global data, see T Zellweger, P Sieger and P Englisch (2015) *Coming Home or Breaking free? A closer look at the succession intentions of next-generation family business members*, University of St Gallen – HSG and EY. Similar

findings, on a narrower and more recent sample of Generation Z successors, are reported by B Chillakuri, J V S Hitesh and K S Srinivas. Getting the next generation ready to take over family business: A Generation Z perspective, *South Asian Journal of Management*, 2022, 29, 92–115.

2 T Zellweger, P Sieger and F Halter (2011) Should I stay or should I go? Career choice intentions of students with family business background, *Journal of Business Venturing*, 26, 521–36.

3 For a summary of this research, see S C Bushardt, M Young and A Bari. Transitioning to management: Challenges and opportunities for the Millennial generation, *Journal of Business Diversity*, 2018, 18 (1).

4 M Young and J J Cater III. Millennials in family firms: Success factors, enhancing firm attractiveness and the changing roles of successors, *Southern Journal of Business and Ethics*, 2019, 11, 157–80.

5 V F Reyna and C J Brainerd. Dual processes in decision making and developmental neuroscience: A Fuzzy-Trace model, *Developmental Review*, 2011, 31. For further detail based on large survey data, see J K Hartshorne and L K Germine. When does cognitive functioning peak? The asynchronous rise and fall of different cognitive abilities across the life span, *Psychological Science*, 2015, 26 (4).

6 J Fryt, M Szczygieł and N Duell. Positive and negative risk-taking: Age patterns and relations to domain-specific risk-taking, *Advances in Life Course Research*, 2022, 54.

8 From dominant leadership to governance: Strengthen systems

1 E Schein. The role of the founder in creating organizational culture, *Organizational Dynamics*, 1983, 12 (1), 13–28.

2 For a very interesting study of how dominant coalitions can assume power over family businesses by using relational ties even when shareholdings are dispersed, see D Ben-Shahar, A Carmeli, E Sulganik and D Weiss. Power and dominant coalitions in family business, *Academy of Management Review*, 2023, 48 (3), 530–55.

3 Contrary to received wisdom, dominant personal leadership and the centralization of power that go with it can have a negative effect in times of crisis. See V K Gupta, S Han, V Nanda and S Silveri. When crisis knocks, call a powerful CEO (or not): Investigating the contingent link between CEO power and firm performance during industry turmoil, *Group and Organization Management*, 2018, 43.

4 For a highly relevant analysis of how family business consultants and family enterprise lawyers can (should) complement each other, see H Krasnow. The family business consultant and the family enterprise lawyer: Some thoughts on a more productive collaboration, *FFI Practitioner*, March 2019.

5 Cf H Korine and P-Y Gomez (2014) *Strong Managers, Strong Owners*, Cambridge University Press, Cambridge.

9 From succession to co-evolution: Grow leaders

1 For example, 2023 survey data for the United States reports that 61 per cent of family businesses do not have written succession plans. Cf Brightstar Capital Partners and Campden Wealth. *The North America Family Business Report 2023*, Brightstar, 2023. brightstarcp.com/family-business-report/ (archived at https://perma.cc/WQB4-26HP)

2 M Filser, S Kraus and S Märk. Psychological aspects of succession in family business management, *Management Research Review*, 2013, 36 (3), 256–77. Cf also M F R Kets de Vries. The dark side of entrepreneurship, *Harvard Business Review*, 1985, 63, 160–67.

3 D J Schepker, A J Nyberg, M D Ulrich and P M Wright. Planning for future leadership: Procedural rationality, formalized succession processes and CEO influence on CEO succession planning, *Academy of Management Journal*, 2018, 61. It is worth pointing out that much of the research in this line of inquiry focuses on listed firms. C-suite succession in family firms is often confounded with generational transition.

4 M K Cabrera-Suarez, D J Garcia-Almeida and P De Saa-Perez. A dynamic network model of the successor's knowledge construction from the resource- and knowledge-based view of the family firm, *Family Business Review*, 2018, 31.

5 Z Zhu and Y Kang. A far-reaching parental love? Co-governance of intergenerational succession and innovation activities in Chinese family firms, *Management and Organization Review*, 2021, 18 (2).

6 For a very interesting discussion of the psychological importance of incumbent support for their successors in the years *preceding* the formal hand over of power, see M Gagné, C Marwick, S Brun de Pontet and C Wrosch. Family business succession: What's motivation got to do with it? *Family Business Review*, 2021, 34, 154–67.

7 The key empirical reference here is T J Quigley and D C Hambrick. When the former CEO stays on as board chair: Effects on successor discretion, strategic change and performance, *Strategic Management Journal*, 2012, 33 (7), 834–59. Quigley and Hambrick show that in the case of publicly listed companies in the dynamic technology sector, the former CEO staying on as board chair has a constraining effect on the successor and a negative effect on performance measures. Similar results have been reported for family businesses: J-P Ahrens,

L Uhlaner, M Woywode and J Zybura. 'Shadow emperor' or 'loyal paladin'? The Janus face of previous owner involvement in family firm successions, *Journal of Family Business Strategy*, 2018, 9 (1), 73–90.

8 Our thinking is echoed in M Katiuska Cabrera-Suárez, D Juan García-Almeida and P De Saá-Pérez. A dynamic network model of the successor's knowledge construction from the resource- and knowledge-based view of the family firm, *Family Business Review*, 2018, 31 (2).

Part Four Navigating the transition: Action

1 Kotter's eight steps to change model is a useful starting point for thinking about transformation. J P Kotter (2011) Leading change: Why transformation efforts fail, *On Change Management*, Harvard Business Review Press, Cambridge, MA.

2 Cf K E Gersick, I Lansberg, M Desjardins and B Dunn. Stages and transitions: Managing change in the family business, *Family Business Review*, 1999, 12, 4.

3 B Dunn. The family factor: The impact of family relationship dynamics on business-owning families during transitions, *Family Business Review*, 1999, 12, 1.

10 Leadership practices: Promote the aspirational and uphold the foundational

1 Z Kunda (1999) *Social Cognition: Making sense of people*, MIT Press, Cambridge, MA. For a narrower take on the question of age, see T D Nelson (ed.) (2002) *Ageism: Stereotyping and prejudice against older persons*, MIT Press, Cambridge, MA.

2 Ubiquitous in society, behavioural norms have a long and rich history in the study of human behaviour. For an early attempt at classification, see J P Gibbs. Norms: The problem of definition and classification, *American Journal of Sociology*, 1965, 70, 586–94. For a summary of more recent research on the topic, see J E Anderson and D Dunning. Behavioral norms: Variants and their identification, *Social and Personality Psychology Compass*, 2014, 8 (12), 721–38.

3 Cf E A Locke and G P Latham (1990) *A Theory of Goal Setting and Task Performance*, Prentice-Hall, Englewood Cliffs, NJ. See also E A Locke and G P Latham. Building a practically useful theory of goal setting and task motivation: A 35-year odyssey, *American Psychologist*, 2002, 57, 705–17.

4 For an interesting look at how retiring leaders disengage from the business and then do or do not re-engage with new projects post retirement see M Gagnè, C Wrosch and S Brun de Pontet. Retiring from the family business: The role of goal adjustment capacities, *Family Business Review*, 2011, 24 (4).

5 Cf K Au, F F Chiang, T A Birtch and Z Ding. Incubating the next generation to venture: The case of a family business in Hong Kong, *Asia Pacific Journal of Management*, 2013, 30.

6 It is worth pausing here to note that 'living up' to the example of the Current Gen can be extremely difficult and sometimes psychologically debilitating for the next generation, particularly when the founder of the business represents the Current Gen. As outlined in Chapter 3 and highlighted in the accompanying fictional case, intergenerational rivalry is real and the next generation may put a great deal of pressure on itself to show that it is as capable as or even more capable than the Current Gen.

7 Cf M C Grosh, E del Ninno, E Tesliuc and A Ouerghi (2008) *For Protection and Promotion: The design and implementation of effective safety nets*, The International Bank for Reconstruction and Development/The World Bank, Washington DC.

8 A Sen. Freedom of choice: Concept and content, *European Economic Review*, 1992, 32.

9 See, for example, C Fernandez-Araoz, et al. 6 traits of strong family businesses, *Harvard Business Review*, June 2019.

11 Transformation initiatives: Launch, build momentum, embed and conclude

1 For an insightful empirical study of the phases of succession transition, see B Murray. The succession transition process: A longitudinal perspective, *Family Business Review*, 2003, 16, 1.

12 Learning opportunities: Understand, discuss, apply and share

1 For a history of one of the oldest family businesses still in existence, see W M Fruin (1983) *Kikkoman: Company, clan and community*, Harvard University Press, Cambridge, MA.

2 Both the self-assessment and the self-reflection are of primary relevance to family business readers, of the current generation and the next generation. Readers or classroom participants who are not members of a business family will not be able to work with these tools in a meaningful way.

3 For precise instructions on how to organize an Oxford-style debate, refer to US Courts. Oxford style debate, US Courts, nd. www.uscourts.gov/about-federal-courts/educational-resources/about-educational-outreach/activity-resources/oxford (archived at https://perma.cc/6KTZ-WSEC)

Epilogue

1 Cf W M Murphy. Reverse mentoring at work: Fostering cross-generational learning and developing Millennial leaders, *Human Resource Management*, 2012, 41 (4), 549–73.

INDEX